"We must never forget that we're AmeriCANS. We, as a nation, have been blessed with a 'can do' spirit that has served us well for over two centuries. In Richard V. Battle's new book, you'll find, not only hope, but the inspiration to keep that AmeriCAN spirit alive and well. And, honestly, couldn't we all use a little hope and inspiration these days?"
—Dreama Denver, award-winning author and wife Bob Denver of "Gilligan's Island" fame

"I have known Richard Battle for a couple of years professionally, and I have always found him well thought out in any conversation. He is a true believer in God and his country. In his book *Made in America by AmeriCANS, not AmeriCAN'TS*, Richard lays it out in his unique style. He points out a problem and then gives us his not-so-common, common-sense solution. He is prolific at pointing out lessons from history and how to grow and learn from them. It is a straightforward book that opens your eyes to the past and the future you want to create. As his dad said, 'What difference will it make in 100 years,' and how Richard explains how we can make a big difference, I know the first step in making things better 100 years from now is getting a copy and reading this book.' God Bless America!
—Al Travis, Host of *Al in The Afternoon* radio show

"You'll have to look really hard to find a book with more gems of wisdom than *Made in America by AmeriCans not AmeriCants*. Richard Battle reminds us that in life, we're either green and growing or ripe and rotting. If you're looking to improve your life both personally and professionally, I highly recommend this book."
—Byrd Baggett, CSP. Author, Professional Speaker

"Once again, with *Made in America by AmeriCANS, not AmeriCANTS*, acclaimed author Richard Battle has taken humanity to new heights of understanding, leadership, and service. For nearly a decade, Richard and I have had conversations about Americanism, a cherished topic for us both. In this book, Richard has distilled the essence of what being an American should be - our sense of hope in the face of adversity, individual achievement, lifelong learning, service to others, and natural humor. Richard reminds us, with great eloquence and solid examples, that we are still one nation – under God. If you are looking for ways to become a better American, you will find them here in this fabulous book."

—Dr. Robert Brescia, Author, AP Government & Politics Teacher, Ethics and Values Professor

"In his book, Richard Battle delivers a powerful defense of the American way of life while providing unique insight for a path forward. He clarifies the thought that 'comparison is the enemy of contentment' while simultaneously encouraging everyone to take action for what extraordinary things they CAN do. Reading about Richard Battle's America is timeless and thought-provoking."

—Bobby Burns, President & CEO of Midland Texas Chamber of Commerce, former three-term Mayor of Midland, and Director of the Shepperd Leadership Institute.

"*Made in America by AmeriCANS not AmeriCANTS* is chock full of ideas to achieve exceptional accomplishments by having a can-do attitude. It reminds me of the Can-Do program I implemented as Mayor of Austin, Texas."

—Ron Mullen, Former Mayor of Austin, Texas

MADE IN AMERICA
BY AmeriCANS NOT AmeriCANTS

MORE COMMON SENSE IN UNCOMMON TIMES

RICHARD V. BATTLE

Headline Books, Inc.
Terra Alta, WV

Made In America by AmeriCANS not AmeriCANTS
More Common Sense in Uncommon Times

by Richard V. Battle

copyright ©2023 Richard V. Battle

To order additional copies of this book or for book publishing information, or to contact the author:

Headline Books, Inc.
P.O. Box 52
Terra Alta, WV 26764
www.HeadlineBooks.com

Tel: 304-789-3001
Email: mybook@headlinebooks.com

ISBN 13: 9781958914021

Library of Congress Control Number: 2022942626

PRINTED IN THE UNITED STATES OF AMERICA

For Leslie-
Thank you for your encouragement and inspiration.

Table of Contents

PREFACE

After publishing *Conquering Life's Course: Common Sense in Chaotic Times* and *Navigating Life's Journey: Common Sense in Uncommon Times*, I thought I had completed my commentary of ideas on life and my cherished Western civilization and American values.

Fate decided otherwise. Between the continued threats of COVID-19, internal and external threats to our freedom, and my radio and television commentary on current events to publicize my speaking efforts and books, a wellspring of inspiration continued providing me material.

I'm grateful to appear weekly with John Rush on *Rush to Reason* on KLZ in Denver and Al Travis (Thielfoldt) on *Al in the Afternoon* on KTOE and other stations in Minnesota. Preparing discussion material each week morphed into essays in this volume.

I'm thankful to work with Burke Allen and Shaili Priya at Allen Media Strategies. They created additional material that sparked ideas for other pieces.

Before I realized it, this work emerged before publishing *Life's Daily Treasure* as my eighth book. Initially, I envisioned a continuation of the theme of the two previously mentioned volumes. However, when I reviewed the articles, I discovered the topics were more focused on our country and culture and less on life lessons utilizing mine and others' examples.

I'm no Thomas Paine, but we live in similar times as when he published *The American Crisis* in 1776. As he stated so eloquently in *The Crisis, Number One*, **"These are the times that**

try men's souls." Additionally, he properly identified human nature's response to prosperity in any part of life, stating, **"what we obtain too cheap, we esteem too lightly: it is dearness only that gives everything its value."**

We Americans have been blessed beyond any people since creation with individual economic and political freedom, living in the most prosperous country in history, and reaping the rewards of peace and plenty.

It is easy to feel our lot is guaranteed because it "has always been that way." The last real mortal threat to the country was World War II before most of us were born. I remember school drills preparing for nuclear attack, but only the Cuban Missile Crisis in 1962 made it seem real.

China, Russia, Islamic extremists, and a socialist push to "transform" our country are severe threats to our freedom and life. A focus on climate, racism, and gender identification is serious to some, silly to others, and a waste of time to other people.

I wrote this humble offering to present ideas for consideration that have worked for our country and people from the beginning. As Thomas Jefferson said so wisely, **"In matters of style, swim with the current; in matters of principle, stand like a rock."**

May we all live like this, preserving principle and advancing our tastes.

INTRODUCTION

This volume adds to my previous life essays celebrating American and Western civilization commonsense values. It began with *Conquering Life's Course: Common Sense in Chaotic Times* and *Navigating Life's Journey: Common Sense in Uncommon Times. Although presented in a unique format, Life's Daily Treasure declares the same values.*

Utilizing stories of others, inspirational quotations, and personal experiences to entertain, inform, encourage, and inspire readers to recognize the gift we inherited from millions of people over hundreds of years who developed a culture resulting in creating the most prosperous country in the history of the world.

I strongly believe in the principles, values, and ideals that founded the United States but recognize all people are imperfect, and some corrupt even the best of societies over time.

Regardless, our founding values are worth defending, preserving, and striving to "form a more perfect union," as advocated as the first purpose in the Preamble to the Constitution of The United States.

This volume and those I previously authored are humble contributions to that effort.

As in two previous volumes, this work includes bite-sized essays illustrating principles and values. Readers can read the articles in any sequence they choose, follow up with additional study as stimulated, and reap the rewards of an expanded mind.

***

In this volume, I separate the chapters into three categories.

Learning is a lifelong opportunity for everyone and a requirement for anyone seeking to fulfill their destiny. It begins before birth and continues at various paces throughout life. Some mistakenly believe learning ends with the conclusion of formal education. Learning should only end with our last breath. There are too many examples of people whose most significant impact occurred in a second or third career or vocation.

That is why I also include learning in the second section on Leading and the third section. If you haven't committed to lifelong learning, I can't encourage you enough to do so.

Learning and Leading others can begin anytime but once commenced, we should inspire and empower others to achieve their fortune, and I'm not referring to only a financial one. Leadership qualities may be inherent, but continual learning will enhance anyone's skills, whether it is or not.

Learning, Leading, and Legacy usually arrive in our consciousness later in our journey when we determine we can best serve others by sharing our wisdom and leading experience with the future. We stand on the shoulders of forbears and ancestors who couldn't conceive our current opportunities. Our responsibility is to train and prepare future generations who will stand on our shoulders.

We will leave the best legacy with continual learning, exercising leadership in every sphere of our influence, and purposefully and uniquely bequeathing what we can for those who come behind us. If we do so, we will leave this earth a life well-lived.

***

Former U.S. Supreme Court Justice Oliver Wendell Holmes may have best stated my hope and objective with these three volumes. "A man's mind is stretched by a new idea or sensation and never shrinks back to its former dimensions."

My hope and earnest desire are for readers to realize one or more ideas from this volume that expands their minds, leads to action, and positively impacts our world today and tomorrow.

Acknowledgments

Any work or effort, such as writing a book, has an army of encouragers directly or indirectly behind its creation, and this one is no different.

Unfortunately, it is impossible to name everyone who contributed positively to my life, but you are appreciated. Realizing some are unknown to me, returning the favor to some of those coming behind me without their awareness is crucial to me.

Words are insufficient to express my appreciation to Logan Cummings, my friend, mentor, and former pastor, whose selfless gift of advice, counsel, and encouragement is priceless to any accomplishments I may achieve.

Many thanks to Charles Larkam, a long-time friend whose encouragement and example have inspired me and countless others.

Thank you to Burke Allen, Shaili Priya, and the Allen Media Strategies team, who represent me professionally but have also become such great friends and cheerleaders of my mission.

I appreciate John Rush, his Rush to Reason radio program, and KLZ radio in Denver for believing in me and granting me a weekly platform to comment on the issues of the day. I'm grateful for his producer, Anne Meurer, who routinely makes me look better than I am.

Thank you to Al Travis Thielfoldt, the king of Southern Minnesota radio, for providing me a microphone weekly as well on his Al in The Afternoon program.

I sincerely appreciate Cathy Teets and the team at Headline Books for her faith in me and this project. Their expertise and contributions were invaluable.

COVER PHOTO STORY

Continuing my tradition of commenting on the cover illustrations of my books, I would like to share my vision of *Made in America by AmeriCANS, not AmeriCANTS* cover.

The image displays four essential components to believers in a strong America and strong AmeriCANS. Individually they are powerful and together promise future success for our beloved country.

The early morning sky with broken clouds reveals hope, the infinite possibilities of the day, and the beauty of creation by our loving Creator.

The rising sun promises an opportunity for each of us to utilize the new day to grow, learn, lead, and leave a legacy maximizing our achievement and contribution to others' futures.

The glorious eagle is soaring freely, grasping and protecting our flag, displaying sacrifice and service to our country and fellow citizens. Millions have served our people in the military, and other forms of public service, creating the gift of freedom blessing our lives.

Our magnificent flag was created upon the birth of our country. It inspired our national anthem when under attack in 1814 and now displays 50 stars for the states and 13 stripes for the original colonies. It communicates freedom to our citizens and others wherever it flies.

And finally, the picture reflects the gratitude for our forebears, the liberty of today, and the hope for a "more perfect union" for tomorrow.

Our ancestors who built the America we enjoy were AmeriCANS. They created a representative republic gifting us individually economic and political freedom beyond anything seen in world history. AmeriCANS create, build, re-create, and re-build with positive attitudes, as this work and history demonstrate.

SECTION ONE

LEARNING

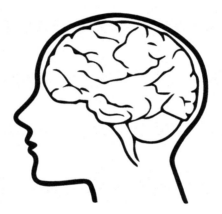

"Those who keep learning will keep rising in life."
—Charles Munger

How We Became AmeriCANS
Instead of AmeriCAN'TS

Today's turmoil can make us forget we are AmeriCANS by birth or naturalization and by our history over 200 years.

Our CAN-DO Attitude is in our genes and makes us exceptional! I also fervently believe we're an extraordinary country by divine providence and the inspiration given to our founders, those who overcame unimaginable obstacles without any thought of "help from the government" to forge our future and gift us freedom very rarely seen by humans in history.

Our heroes and benefactors were not perfect, but overcame their limitations to achieve tremendous accomplishments. They built a civilization where there wasn't one, contributed to the betterment of people where there was one, and enabled individuals to pursue their dreams when, how, and where they wanted to live.

***

There are many more examples of our collective achievements than I can cite here. I believe they prove providence's touch and an inherent can-do attitude in our people.

While he never became an American, Christopher Columbus set the precedent of a can-do attitude with his relentless persistence of achieving his vision of a shortcut to Asia. He wasn't any more perfect than any hero but lived more courageously than any of his critics.

The Pilgrims risked everything with no hope of returning to Europe, sailing for the Americas in 1620. They endured great hardships and suffered staggering losses but established a permanent foothold for Western civilization at Plymouth in 1620.

As the colonies grew and prospered, they yearned for better representation and freedom not extended by England. The Boston Tea Party in 1773, the shot heard around the world at Lexington and Concord on April 19, 1775, The Declaration of Independence, and General George Washington crossing the Delaware River on Christmas 1776 were highlights of a seven-year war of independence.

The U.S. Constitution in 1787, which is still the longest-serving governing document, codified individual and state's rights and **delegated specific and limited power** to a new federal governing body. Unfortunately, the child continues to seize power from the parent and now acts as the dominant party as was never intended.

The Bill of Rights enumerated individual rights and restricted the government's power further. It has protected us for two centuries but is under attack as never before today.

***

As the country grew and the 19th century dawned, citizens lived their dreams freely. They contributed to the republican experiment knowing freedom would not survive without everyone sharing their talents with their friends and neighbors.

The Lewis and Clark expedition in 1804 to explore the Louisiana Purchase might as well have been a trip to the moon. Lasting two years, without any communication or support from their countrymen, they traveled to the Pacific Ocean and back, losing only one man. Sacagawea, a young Shoshone woman, enabled them to peacefully interact with Native American tribes and succeed in their mission.

Before entering the United States, Texans fought their war of independence against Mexico. Sacrificing for their friends and relatives, men at The Alamo fought to the death, and Texans avenged their deaths at San Jacinto, securing the republic for nine years.

The most significant blemish in the American experiment was slavery. Though practiced throughout time and across the world, it is an unacceptable institution. The founders reluctantly relented to secure the necessary commitment from all 13 colonies to win independence. The Civil War saw more than 600,000 Americans die to extinguish slavery in the United States.

The wagon trains of pioneers settling the West again demonstrated people's independent and optimistic attitude, willing to risk everything with no support from governments or those they left behind pursuing better lives and futures. Weather, lack of food and water, native and criminal attacks, and illness reduced the numbers of those who reached their destination. Those who did were strengthened from experience and emboldened to pursue loftier achievements.

***

The 20th century dawned with the industrial revolution completely underway. Americans built their accomplishments on the successful and unsuccessful experiences of those before them.

The 1918 Spanish Flu epidemic ravaged the country with sickness and death. Families faced disease and loss with no social safety net as would develop later. Necessity forced people to toughen up for the challenge. Illustrating the old expression "that which doesn't kill us makes us stronger," survivors were prepared for more challenges in the future.

The 1920s roared with prosperity and ended with economic hardship as the Great Depression began. Again, people faced difficult times without hope for relief. Overcoming the difficulties strengthened individuals' resolve and confidence that they could face almost anything and survive.

Sandwiched around the epidemic and depression, World War I and II threatened the country's mortality and civilization.

People rallied together, and each person found their place to contribute to the effort to protect and further the life of the United States. Again, each victory bolstered everyone and thus the people and, therefore, the country itself.

Post-World War II saw tremendous growth and prosperity for the country, culture, and the people.

President Ronald Reagan's optimistic attitude and rhetoric came at a time of discouragement among the people and inspired the country to achieve a decade of peace and prosperity. Once, I was fortunate to hear one of his speeches in person. Then, and on television, he made everyone feel as if he or she was the only person being spoken to by the Great Communicator, as Reagan came to be called.

***

Despite the 9/11 attacks, a long period of global war, financial upheavals, social justice campaigns, and other setbacks, the United States, in the 21st century, is still the country people around the world look to for leadership and example.

So many people want what Americans possess. They stream illegally across the border at unprecedented levels risking everything, including their lives. Others respect our laws and immigrate legally, desiring to assimilate into our culture and improving the trajectory of their families' futures.

Nowhere do people have more individual liberty and economic and political freedom than we who live in the United States. We are free to achieve great dreams that benefit all people today and in the future.

We must remember: there is no political freedom without economic freedom. Those who attack private property desiring to redistribute it in the name of "equity" threaten centuries of building and success for an ideology that only succeeds in theory.

***

As in every other example, those selling equity and social justice believe it will be different this time. We're smarter than those who tried to build a utopia in other times and places. They refuse to accept the problem is not who is leading the revolution but the utopian idealism itself.

Their fatal flaw is a knowing or unknowing misunderstanding of human nature. They believe human nature is evolving, and with their intervention, the selfless, ideal utopia will arrive.

Hundreds of millions of people murdered during other countries' pursuits of nirvana affirm human nature has not changed. Regardless of who is leading a government, it will never change.

If my assertion is correct, **why would we throw away what has worked very well, though imperfectly, for what the millions who rush to America at the earliest opportunity can't escape quickly enough?**

As Thomas Sowell expertly said, "Much of the social history of the Western world over the past three decades has involved replacing what worked with what sounded good."

The immortal philosopher Yogi Berra said it differently, "In theory, there is no difference in theory and practice. In practice, there is."

AmeriCANS lead us to victory and achievement. AmeriCANT'S lead us to defeat and dishonor!

***

So, what must we do to preserve our AmeriCAN attitude and resist those who would sentence us to a future as AmeriCANT'S?

1. We should revere our unique gift of remembering and studying the history of our families and ancestors.
2. We should commit to preserving our CAN-DO spirit and teach our children what it is and why it is imperative for their and successive generations.
3. We should RETURN THE FAVOR of the gift we received to those who come behind us. All who sacrificed and contributed to our heritage of individual freedom will have done so in vain if we allow others to extinguish it.

4. We MUST:
   - **Stand up** and actively participate in governance.
   - **Show up** when we can and where we can to support those fighting to protect our interests.
   - **Speak up** to let our voices influence policy.
   - **Stay up** in the fight. There will be no rest until we neutralize the current threat. It may take longer than we like, but the resulting resumption of unthreatened freedom will be worth the price for us and our children.

No one can do everything, but each of us can do one thing!

It is WE, THE PEOPLE, who make America! NOT the government!

Be encouraged our children and America are worth the effort, and encourage others!

We ONLY lose if we quit.

So as with all things, I encourage everyone to Aim High, Work Hard, and NEVER Quit! ®

Has Human Nature Evolved?
If not, What Difference
Does it Make In Our Lives?

Has human nature progressed over the centuries or retained its native instincts? Intellectuals pronounce man's improvements because they are essential to adopting and promoting moral relativism.

I believe our view on the progress of humanity over the centuries and its likelihood of continued improvement vs. its consistency from the beginning of time to the present and through the future is the basis for our view on life's most critical issues. My hope is this essay will inspire you to think and reflect about your beliefs and why to provide you a foundational conviction to base future decisions.

If humanity has advanced, it is easy to discard ancient principles because they no longer apply to humans who have surpassed their application.

What does science say? Are we asking objective science unencumbered by obligations to benefactors or those scientists bought by grants and governments predisposed to results matching their agendas?

If we can't trust science, the media, or current academia, is there any source we can depend on for an unbiased answer?

***

I would submit that we can find all of the validation we need about man's past, present, and future nature in *The Bible*.

Before you disregard my argument, I'm not advocating the Bible's theology in this piece, but its contents as literature.

My premise is even if the theology isn't applicable, its writers based their stories on how humans behaved when the Bible was authored thousands of years ago.

Avoiding responsibility was plainly displayed in Genesis 3 when God confronted Eve about eating the forbidden fruit. She immediately, and without hesitation, blamed the serpent. No better was Adam, who blamed Eve when it was his turn to answer for the transgression.

Ask any young child what happened when something breaks, and they instinctively, without hesitation, state, "I didn't do it." Our natural reaction is to avoid responsibility. It takes learning, training, and the ability to think about the implications beyond an incident to accept responsibility for our actions.

***

Jealousy and envy are displayed repeatedly in scripture. Cain killing Abel and Jacob stealing Esau's birthright and inheritance, also in Genesis, are prime examples.

You can hardly find a television or motion picture whose plots don't include one or more characters who act out of envy. Not to be outdone are commercials whose sole function is to stimulate product purchases to enhance your life by making yourself better than others because you are "entitled" and "deserve it."

Wouldn't we learn over time the useless energy and money wasted feeling jealousy and envy? Despite faith-based and secular programs galore, human instinct contains covetousness for what we don't have instead of gratitude for what we do have.

***

Ambition is another human instinct we see displayed in every area of life. We see countless examples of individuals who desire more regardless of the damage they might cause others in families, businesses, religious organizations, and even charitable causes.

David was King of Israel and could obtain anything he desired by mere command. Despite his bountiful possessions, 2 Samuel tells us, he was overcome with the ambition to possess a beautiful woman he spied bathing on a rooftop from his palace. When he was informed Bathsheba was the wife of Uriah, one of his captains, David proceeded to command her presence, instigated an affair, and had Uriah killed to enable their marriage.

How often do we see today stories of people who have virtually everything but destroy their and others' lives to obtain something they do not control? Wouldn't we think those with the most belongings, intelligence, and knowledge would be able to control their ambitions?

***

Those are but three examples of an untold number in scripture or other ancient texts of human instincts from the past we see every day in the present. If human behavior hasn't changed from thousands of years ago to now, is there any reason to believe it will vary from now into the future?

I contend human nature has not changed from the beginning and will not change from now into the future.

But you say we have made progress in many areas over the centuries. That is correct. Our technological advancements are mind-boggling, but our instincts are the same. Said better by Dr. Logan Cummings, "Mankind is ever advancing, yet man is ever the same."

***

If my argument is correct, it has a monumental impact on our thinking on history, present actions, and the future.

***

Those who argue man has and is evolving discount history because they believe humanity is different today than in past centuries. This supposed progression makes past texts and principles invalid because they don't apply to the people of today or tomorrow.

If yesterday's philosophies and historical precedence don't apply to today's issues, then tomorrow's issues can't be solved by today's decisions. That means all decisions are made in the vacuum of today's knowledge only. How do we learn from history if it doesn't apply to today? How do we hold people accountable if we're different people tomorrow from today?

If decisions are dependable only today, how do we proceed as an orderly society? The answer is we don't, which is what some ambitious people desire. They want to rule people creating chaos and positioning themselves as the only ones capable of solving the day's issues when, in reality, they proceed from one chaotic problem to another to stimulate demand for their continual leadership. In the meantime, the people are whipsawed back and forth, never planning their futures confidently.

***

Suppose human nature is the same as the beginning of humanity. In that case, it means ancient philosophers, Biblical writers, and America's founders who spoke and composed the Declaration of Independence and U.S. Constitution spoke not only to the people of their day but also to people of every day in the present and future.

We can learn from the wisdom of the ages to avoid the unavoidable mistakes and failures from learning on our own. We can trust foundational principles, which provide us with a reliable bulwark to make our decisions. Living in an environment with multi-generational laws and regulations enables us to live more freely because of fewer interactions with bureaucracies enforcing fluid rules and constantly appearing politicians to tell us what changes they made for our benefit.

***

Yes, I believe *The Bible* theologically in addition to it as literature. Additionally, I believe its affirmation of the constancy of human nature enhances its credibility as the divine Word of God. However, you do not have to do so to agree with my premise here.

I also believe *The Declaration of Independence* and *the Constitution* of the United States are as valid today as the day they were published because of the natural consistency of humanity.

We can learn much from these documents, Greek philosophers, and all the wisdom of those who came before us if we're wise enough to embrace them.

Based on two old sayings, I tell people, **If hindsight is 20-20, and experience is the best teacher, why won't the people who have neither listen to the people who have both?**

***

Our past is under a withering attack today. Sir Winston Churchill's modification of the original quote stated, "Those who fail to learn from history are doomed to repeat it."

Our choice is to abandon our history and doom our children and descendants to an unstable future at best or retain the vast knowledge accumulated over the ages to preserve our present and improve the destiny of those who come behind us.

Forgoing historical knowledge leads to the inevitable and comprehensive destruction of civilization's gains and dooms our descendants to an unknown and insecure future.

Honoring the sacrifices of previous generations by embracing the gift of knowledge they left us will inspire us to enhance it with our imprint. Passing past knowledge to those in the future returns the favor to those on whose shoulders we stand and serves as an example to the current generation of their responsibility to build and extend it further.

The choice today is ours, and the impact of our decision is the future.

Three (3) 'Tudes to Living a Terrific Life in Tough Times

Has anyone ever accused you of having a "'tude"?

If you're unfamiliar with the term, you're not alone. Merriam-Webster online defines a "'tude" as "a cocky or arrogant attitude."[1]

***

I believe we can have a confident but not cocky attitude, including three components leading to a remarkable life in tough times. These three factors cost nothing and always work, and we can choose to implement them every day.

Conversely, some people choose not to adopt one or more of them, and life is a more rigorous experience for them because of their choices.

***

While I write this during the 2020 COVID-19 pandemic, my life experience reinforces my final adoption and reliance on these elements to benefit me daily. Financial devastation, divorce, heart procedures, cancer, and losing my only son were more significant challenges than I wish I had endured. They tested and proved the validity and essentialness of these three "'tudes."

They helped others before me. They help me consistently. And they will help you if you embrace them in your life daily!

***

The first "'tude" that will positively change you is **Gratitude** for everything you have received in life.

Our human tendency is to focus on what we would like but don't have. Observing others with the things we desire exacerbates our self-pity.

Why should so-and-so have that and I don't? When we focus on what we don't have, we never think of what we have the person we are envious of does not have. We zero in on only what we want and want now!

There is a quixotic quest by some today to achieve total equality. It is not merely foolish but dangerous as it promotes greed, envy, and covetousness. It doesn't matter who leads the government. No human can deliver equality to other humans period! Some people are taller, better looking, thinner, more prosperous, live in a better environment, and will live longer, regardless of who you vote for in the next election. Wishing we had something we don't have will only lead to unhappiness.

When we're grateful for what we have, we see we have more than many others. We also observe others who have less than we do but strive to improve themselves and their families for the future. Our country was founded by and is full of examples of people who overcame early obstacles and reached unfathomable heights.

Helen Keller was born in 1880. When she was less than two years old, she lost her sight and hearing. Families in those days cast aside their loved ones with disabilities. Fortunately, Helen's family hired Anne Sullivan to teach her braille.

Helen focused on her brain and her desire to live a fulfilling life. She was the first deaf-blind person to earn a bachelor's degree. Her determination to communicate as conventionally as possible led her to speak and lecture about her life.

Her messages of good cheer and hope inspired countless individuals. *If Helen could overcome her obstacles,* they would realize, *why can't I?*

She traveled extensively, authored twelve books, and participated in the political activities of the period.

Helen Keller inspires all to learn of her story of gratitude, determination, and contributions to the world.

***

The second "'tude" is closely related to gratitude. Every day, we choose our **Attitude**. Our choice influences the rest of the day as much as any other factor in life.

We can choose to see the negative in every aspect of the day. When we do so, we will reap the negative part of every event we experience. Not only will we make ourselves miserable, but also we will make everyone we encounter miserable as well. If we repeat this choice often enough, we shouldn't be surprised when others don't want to associate with us. NO ONE wants to hang around a negative person!

On the other hand, when we look for the positive in the day's circumstances, we will see the positive side of each one of them. We will be happier, and our attitude will infect others. Wouldn't you instead spend time with a positive person?

Henry Ford said, "There are those who think they can, and those who think they can't. They're both right." You will be more successful and happier in life when you maintain a positive attitude!

Viktor Frankl found himself in a Nazi concentration camp during World War II. As an experienced neurologist and psychiatrist, observing everything in prison came naturally to him. He discovered man's last freedom was to choose his response in any circumstance. Those surviving the camp and war confirmed his conclusion that prisoners with a positive outlook on life escaped death at a much greater rate than those with opposing perspectives.

***

The third "'tude" leading to an extraordinary life is **Servitude**. I'm referring to voluntarily helping others by utilizing the gifts you have been given.

Our human tendency is to focus on ourselves. When I have found myself exercising this choice, I am less happy. There is no level of success that is satisfactory when we obsess about ourselves. We will always want more and better.

When we focus on serving others, we lose all negative thoughts about ourselves. When we dedicate our hearts to service, we are repeatedly engulfed with satisfaction and achievement. The joy and pleasure we experience are intoxicating. They lead to continued endeavors that never fail to fulfill our hearts.

Soon we learn the excellent feeling of service is superior to the sense of defeat when we focus on only our self-interests.

C. William "Bill" Brownfield wrote the creed for The United States Junior Chamber of Commerce in 1947. Its concluding line states, "Service to humanity is the best work of life!" I believe my fellow members cherished that verse and what it represented based on the countless projects conducted to improve communities and individuals around the country for many years. To this day, we live that statement daily.

People often hesitate to serve others because they don't believe they can contribute enough to make it worth the effort. Albert Schweitzer said, "One person can and does make a difference."

Former President John F. Kennedy said, "One person can make a difference, and everyone should try." Our daily choice is to choose to help others and make an effort. My experience tells me you will be surprised looking back on your impact.

***

What Can We Do Today to Experience a Terrific Life?
1. Focus on what you have, not what you don't have.
2. **Be grateful for what you have.**
3. Choose to live daily with a **Positive Attitude**.

4. Think about how you can **serve others** instead of focusing on only yourself.
5. Be an example of the 3 "'tudes" to others!

Life is ours to choose every day. Our choices influence our attitude and impact much more than circumstances affect our lives. We should resolve today to make positive choices and lead by example.

1 - Merriam-Webster online dictionary, www.merriam-webster.com.

NOBODY SAID LIFE
WOULDN'T BE SEMI-TOUGH?

I know. You heard this somewhere before. This title slightly alters the classic line in the 1977 football movie *Semi-Tough*. The protagonist, Billy Clyde Puckett, often tells whoever is within earshot, "Well, nobody said it wasn't going to be semi-tough."

My contention is the quote applies to life "its own self" to borrow another quote from the book's author, Dan Jenkins.

***

In a life filled with semi-tough moments, we can never receive enough encouragement to help us face whatever displaces our daily routines with stress, adversity, and discomfort. I like to say "boring is good," not to prefer boredom daily but in appreciation of a lack of negativity in a day.

As I wrote in *Conquering Life's Course*, "Encouragement is the Greatest Gift We Can Give Anyone." It doesn't cost us anything. We never know when a positive word may transform someone's life from a negative trajectory to one of optimism and enthusiasm. People like to associate with positive people, and you will attract more people to you when you provide them encouraging words instead of discouragement.

***

In the midst of what everyone would argue was one of the most unusual years anyone could remember, Madison Cawthorn was twenty-five years old when he burst into the public eye in 2020. Madison suffered partial paralysis when he was eighteen years old but has not allowed it to deter the pursuit of his dreams.

Madison first gained attention when he defeated a more-experienced, older individual endorsed by the United States President in the primary for a U.S. Congressional seat.

His speech at his party's convention vaulted him into a different esteem level by a significant portion of the public. His speech inspired hope for the country and his generation. Madison's closing was dramatic and affirmed the patriotism of millions.

On a stage in front of several flags, Madison spoke from his wheelchair. Two gentlemen suddenly appeared and stood next to him. They reached down, helped Madison stand in front of his chair, and then retired from the picture.

Madison proclaimed his love for the United States and our flag. He declared, "I stand for America," in a display of commitment those of us who can easily stand may not fully appreciate.

While many people question the generation coming of age in the 2020s, Madison exhibits enthusiasm, optimism, faith, and hope for the United States' future success. His example of overcoming his accident, and his service to help others, is exemplary and worthy of emulation by people of all ages.

***

While Madison's story is still unfolding, he illustrates positively the warning given by Charles R. Swindoll, "**Life is 10% what happens to you and 90% how you react to it.**" He does not permit his accident or physical limitation to restrict his life's mission.

In every circumstance in life, we choose how we respond. When everything is going well, replies are simple and easy to select. When difficulty arises, our test begins, and our responses are more complex and essential.

Unfortunately, we all make poor choices in our lives. Some lead to a lifetime of loss as the one decision propels the traveler farther down the chosen path. Other times, we recognize our shortcomings and desire to stop, turn around, and return to our previously positive trail.

Focusing on our guilt in making a mistake can entrap us into a life limited by one choice. We forfeit our future impact and success when we sentence ourselves to metaphorical jail for our misstep. More importantly, our lack of continued development and influence deprives anyone we may positively touch from our contributions to the quality of their lives.

However, if we overcome guilt from our negative choice and return to a productive life, the detour and its effects are soon forgotten. Winston Churchill's words encourage us to shake off the shackles of guilt and resume our positive efforts when he said, "**Success is not final; failure is not fatal:** it is the courage to continue that counts."

***

How Do We Respond to our Semi-Tough Life Moments?
1. Recognize everyone experiences challenging moments in life.
2. Realize our response to the event or our choice is more important than what happened.
3. Recall Winston Churchill's warning "failure is not fatal" if you find you have made a poor decision.
4. Remember that we all are examples to others by our actions, whether we want to be or not.
5. Return to maximizing every day to grow and impact others.
6. Reassure others that it is still possible for them to return to a positive path.
7. Reach for the stars! Whatever your dreams are, pursue them vigorously!

***

Every day of our lives is a blessing. We should use them to grow into our destiny and positively impact others' lives. Our paths are seldom linear, but we can always return to the proper one as long as we breathe.

SOME DAYS YOU'RE THE PIGEON ...
DEALING WITH "ONE OF THOSE DAYS"

When was the last time you had "one of those days?" How did you respond to it? Can you laugh about it now?

***

My college fraternity intramural basketball team signed up to play in a charity tournament in East Austin, Texas. We thought it would be a local tournament, and we could compete with our 6'7" junior college all-star center, my 6'4" roommate and me at 6'3" at forward, and two crackerjack guards. We showed up for our early Saturday morning game with our Friday night partying as our only preparation. Some of us had jerseys, and the rest didn't. We didn't even have one ball to warm up with, but I think most of us were more interested in recovering from Friday night than playing basketball.

We looked no further than the parking lot to locate our opponent in the first game. Instead of rolling up in individual cars, they arrived in their team bus with fire in their eyes.

They were a semi-professional team from the Dallas area using this tournament as a warm-up for bigger and better things individually and their team. Like Dorothy, we realized we weren't in Kansas anymore.

They graciously loaned us a ball to warm up out of a large bag of balls. We strained to appear worthy of their time.

When we went to the center circle for the opening jump ball, their 7'0" center looked down on our star, and a 6'9" athletic specimen tapped my shoulder, telling his teammates he "had me." Truer words were never spoken.

The only good news is the few fans in attendance rooted for us because we were so overmatched. Rooted may be a generous term as I remember them laughing at us more than applauding our play.

When the final buzzer sounded, we were on the losing end of a 32-112 score. Thankfully, it wasn't worse! I don't remember scoring much, but there weren't many scores for us to remember. After we shook hands, I'm sure the other team laughed their way off of the court.

We were eliminated in our next game despite our inspired effort while the semi-pros rolled the field, winning the tournament. Our consolation was part of our entry fee went to charity. It was one of those days.

***

One of the advantages of maturing is learning to put life events into perspective. When we're immature, at any age, most disruptive events will set our hair on fire, figuratively speaking.

As you can imagine, I've been able to laugh about my worst sports beatdown for many years. It illustrates the importance of categorizing our life events and knowing what is most important and what isn't as severe in our life.

I've experienced and previously written about many of the challenges in my life. They include the devastating loss of my only son. While I have found humor in heart procedures and cancer treatments, among others, I will never find it in my son's passing.

***

Fortunately, most of our day-to-day challenges are not as severe, and we can find humor in them if our attitude and maturity have prepared us.

Most of you have heard one or more of the following expressions, which humorously express life's ups and downs.

Some days you eat the bear, and some days the bear eats you.
Some days you're the hammer, and some days you're the nail.
Some days you're the pigeon, and some days you're the statue.
Some days you're the windshield, and some days you're the bug.

There are more sayings like these, and you probably know some of them as well.

***

Challenges subject us to decision pressures that hinder our thought process. I know my worst decisions were made under pressure and to "get out of the trap." Once I learned to consider each decision's example and precedent, I found myself making better choices for the short and long term.

Instead of someone using a prior choice to abuse me in the future, I could use my previous decisions as a foundation. They provided me sure footing going forward. I even experienced fewer challenges because my prior choices dissuaded people from approaching me. After all, they knew the decision they would receive.

***

What are seven things we can do to prepare ourselves to best deal with "one of those days" and handle life's challenges?

1. We should **set our Expectations** about the certainty that tough times are part of life.
2. We should **place all setbacks in their proper Perspective.** If possible, **take Time to get away from a challenge until you can better face it, but don't hide from it.**
3. Dr. Robert H. Schuller provided me a great lesson, "**If you have a problem that you can write a check to solve, you don't have a problem, but an expense.**"

4. **The better lifelong learners and thinkers we are, the better and more Alternative Solutions we'll have to consider implementing.**
5. **Consider Example** and **Precedence in any decision you consider.**
6. We should **Learn the lesson from every loss, so we don't have to suffer twice to learn one lesson.**

***

We should cherish every day without a setback or challenge. As I tell people, boring is good.

When "one of those days" does show up, face it head-on. Things are rarely as bad as they appear, and once solved, it's easy to realize.

Finally, John Wayne's words of encouragement still ring true. "When the road looks rough ahead, remember the 'Man upstairs' and the word HOPE. Hang onto both and 'tough it out.'"

It's About Time

Have you ever found yourself so busy time escaped you? Did you ever slow down long enough to recognize it where others have not? Spending some time recognizing time's importance, different intervals, and the impact of our uses of it is extremely valuable.

***

Time is fickle. Each of us receives one second at a time and chooses how we utilize it. Sometimes we are efficient and productive, and often we waste it as if it is available endlessly.

None of us know the number of seconds we will receive on this earth. If we did, we could better determine what time to contribute our mark on the world and what time to enjoy leisure.

We are left to navigate our journey utilizing the time we live, which results in the difference we make in others' lives.

Time exists in the three periods of past, present, and future. It fascinates me how we can live in one segment but have the other two disproportionately influence our lives.

I've written before, but it bears repeating, the wise words I first heard at a Promisekeepers meeting in 1996. Dr. Haddon Robinson said, "Time is our enemy disguised as our friend." It was a profound statement then and has only grown more so over the years.

***

We cannot change what happened in the **past**, but it is striking how it impacts our present and future.

Fondly remembering good times is natural and healthy, but if we live on past glories or failures, we can become trapped and cease our growth and impact on the future.

Past successes fade away and are less impactful if they fail to produce future achievements.

Society burdens us with guilt for past failures, constraining our present and future contributions to others.

My friend, author-speaker Byrd Baggett, advises us, "the past doesn't have a future, but you do." He provides us with a wise perspective for looking in our rear-view mirror.

Learning from our experiences and those of others is the healthiest use of the past. How we view the past is our daily choice in the present.

***

Likewise, our hope for the **future** is always enticing and out of reach. It reminds me of the bar sign saying, "free beer tomorrow." The prize is ever elusive.

Longing and dreaming for what we want in the future obscures our appreciation for what we have in the present. It also distracts us from our opportunities and responsibilities.

Every day we walk into an unknown and uncertain future. Our lack of control often creates worry, fear, and anxiety. Where we place our Hope for peace is our most important decision in life.

When our hopes and dreams are beyond our grasp, our only course is to take incremental steps today and continue to prepare for future action.

Waiting for tomorrow exposes our patience or lack thereof. If we become patient, we will maximize our present, but impatience will lead us to waste today dreaming about our destiny.

***

The only time we can impact is the **present**. Our past prepares us, and our future dreams drive us, but our moment is now.

Because the present is the only time where we can act, it exerts pressure on us. Expectations of others and a self-inflicted drive to succeed add to the importance of maximizing each breath we have on this earth.

We know every second is a fleeting opportunity, but procrastination tugs on our sleeves. It is an easy habit to develop. Mark Twain, who was never known to enjoy hard work, famously encouraged people to "Never put off until tomorrow what you can do the day after tomorrow."

Leisure time is always seductive. The wisdom of the ages proves hard work earlier in life leads to more pleasant days later. Conversely, when individuals prioritize recreation first, life will be more difficult later.

Benjamin Franklin wisely advises all to "Never put off until tomorrow what you can do today." While delaying action feels good in the short term, there is no substitute for the feeling of completing a task ahead of a deadline and enjoying the freedom and relaxation from the accomplishment.

Auto dealers and athletes are great examples of properly focusing their attention on the "moment" to succeed. When we're shopping for cars, dealers don't care if we bought a car yesterday or might buy one tomorrow. They only care if we will "today." Similarly, no previous or future shot matters when a golfer is over the ball. Just the current shot is consequential at that time.

But we have to beware of a trap today also. Pop culture loves the present but disregards the past and future. Its philosophy is "if it feels good, do it" and "eat, drink and be merry for tomorrow we die." Its celebrated styles and fads come-and-go, and those who attempt inclusion in its club are always chasing its next move. Living in its realm is like living in a house built on shifting sand. It is not something to trust, but its seductiveness entraps untold numbers.

***

Physically, we always live in the present. It is only in our mind we allow the past to trap us or the future to distract us. The better we can manage all three time periods, the more fulfilling our lives will be, and the more they will impact others.

***

Healthy perspectives on time.
1. Learn the lessons from our past successes and failures.
2. Study history for the lessons others can teach us.
3. Don't let past failures trap us into limiting our future efforts.
4. Dream big for our future, but keep it in proper perspective to avoid diverting from today's action.
5. Live today to the fullest and prepare for tomorrow's opportunities to build the future.
6. Influence others to maximize their past, present, and future.
7. Until our final breath, we will have opportunities in front of us and choices to make.

***

We should honor and learn from the past, live and contribute in the present, and hope and prepare for the future.

As I wrote in *The Four-Letter Word that Builds Character* in 2006, "What you do in the present will create a past that will greatly influence your opportunities and dreams in the future."

Remember, there is no guarantee of our next breath. We should not delay rearranging our activities to maximize each moment.

Tick-tock, tick-tock, tick-tock...

WHAT'S THE POINT?
YES, THERE IS A POINT!

Whether we experience a personal loss or challenge or find ourselves in the middle of a pandemic, life can be hazardous at times. Some people find themselves wondering if life is worth it? What's the point?

Some decide to "punch out" and end their life on Earth. They mistakenly believe it will end their pain. I would disagree, but it is my opinion. What it will most certainly do is devastate all who care for that individual.

Let me reassure you. There is a point to our lives that is larger than we are and transcends our lifetime on the planet.

***

Whether we realize it or not, each of us makes three far-reaching choices every day that write our life story. Thankfully, we can survive poor decisions and live to select better ones.

First, it is our choice every day how we approach life. We can't grow or positively impact anyone with a negative attitude. Additionally, enjoying life requires a positive outlook. No one wants to be around a negative person, but everyone wants to associate with positive people.

Viktor Frankl was a psychiatrist, among other achievements, who found himself in a Nazi concentration camp during World War II. It was a place he could observe how people responded to man's humanity to man. Frankl discovered man's last freedom was to choose how to respond to any situation. He observed that people with optimistic attitudes survived their imprisonment at much higher rates than those with negative outlooks on their existence.

He recognized "those who have a why to live can bear almost any how." Our purpose complements our attitude to create a significant barrier to destruction and a potent drive to live and produce positive accomplishments.

Frankl wrote *Man's Search for Meaning* among his thirty-nine books and spent the next fifty years teaching and sharing the lessons he learned to help other people achieve more fulfilling lives.

***

Second, we should help who we can, where we can, how we can. Life can often be difficult, and it is more so alone. We may never know the full impact of our efforts, but that is no reason not to make even the slightest attempt wherever we find the opportunity.

Betsie and Corrie ten Boom were sisters who also found themselves in a concentration camp during World War II because of their efforts to hide Jewish people from the Nazis. Their faith helped them endure physical, emotional, and psychological suffering, but only Corrie survived the ordeal.

Betsie's faith was mightier than her body, but she observed before passing from this lifetime, "there is no pit so deep that He is not deeper still."

Corrie dedicated the remaining years of her life to traveling the world to tell the story of Betsie's and her experience and God's provision for them in every circumstance. She authored several books focusing on God's love, forgiveness, and hope. Her example illustrates how God can turn loss and failure into service and success in anyone's life.

***

Third, it is never too late to choose the right path. Life is full of pathways to select for our life's journey, and distractions lure many of us onto ones attractive immediately but destructive if we remain on them. If we're wise or fortunate, we will find our way onto a positive route and follow it faithfully.

Saul of Tarsus had the world in the palm of his hands. He belonged to the right group, was educated, and demonstrated his worthiness through his actions. As he soon discovered, his path was fruitful for a breath in the span of time but disastrous in the expanse of eternity.

Unexpectedly and involuntarily, Saul found himself on the ground while traveling. He discovered the way he previously despised was now his proper path. Saul sacrificed his worldly position for one full of challenges beyond most of our comprehension. After changing his name and becoming the Apostle Paul and accepting his new mission and track, he became the recipient of attacks instead of the deliverer.

Paul was persecuted, beaten, shipwrecked, stoned, left for dead, and experienced danger repeatedly. Despite his suffering, he learned to be content in life in any condition. He recognized his purpose beyond himself. His example is a lesson for all of us that we have a purpose in life beyond ourselves.

***

**What 3 Choices do we make every day
that write our life's story?**

1. We choose our attitude in how we approach the day and life.
2. We choose whether or not we help people whom we can, where we are, and how we can.
3. We choose our path and whether it is the best one for our lifetime and eternity.

***

What we do today, tomorrow, and the rest of our tomorrows is more important than what we did yesterday.

It's our choice every day!

How Can We Succeed Like
Tom Brady in Any Undertaking?

What does Tom Brady know that we can implement to achieve our goals and dreams?

***

Tom Brady impresses us with his athleticism. His ability to consistently perform at championship levels is outstanding.

Whether you watched him attain GOAT (Greatest of All Time) status or not, you most likely know of his championship feats in the National Football League (NFL). To date, he has played in ten Super Bowl championship games, winning seven. No one in the history of the game can match his success.

Is it possible for us to perform at his level in our life? Absolutely! What can we learn from him to attain our life dreams?

Tom Brady did not win any of his Super Bowls on game day. And we won't achieve our goals on the day of attainment either. I'll submit he won seven Super Bowls and any future achievements he realizes many days before they occurred. We win before game day too!

His path began innocently one day with an initial spark that grew into a fire in his heart and mind.

He is a winner because he follows the seven steps below, and we win when we do likewise. Looking back, when I didn't follow them, I fell short of my goals. When I followed the steps, I succeeded every time.

***

How, you ask? The formula is simple, but execution separates championship performance from typical results.

First, we must **make a Choice**. Too easy, you say? As Yogi Berra said, "If you don't know where you're going, you'll end up someplace else." More often than not, we don't achieve something because we never chose to pursue it.

We must first have a **vision** of where we want to go. Recently maligned Christopher Columbus had a specific idea to find a shorter route to the Far East. Even though he did not achieve his dream, he completed more than he imagined, finding what they called The New World. He affirmed, "If you set a goal, you will achieve more even if you don't attain it than if you set no goal."

We must make the initial choice leading to success, but as we'll see shortly, we must also make reaffirming choices every day until we win the championship.

***

Second, we must choose to take a **Chance.** No institution on this earth will eliminate life's **risks.** Winners take risks because their desire for something better in life is more significant than their fear of failure or regret.

We waste our vision until we choose to risk where we are for where we want to go.

***

Third, we must **Change** our behavior. There is no change on Earth without **action**, and we must act on our vision and its risk to propel us toward the life we desire.

Some people believe changing their routine is a four-letter word. Their comfort is more significant than their desire for something else. There is no shame in achieving and remaining at a level of contentment, but it is incompatible with people desiring more during their life.

***

Fourth, we must **Channel** our energy narrowly to **focus** on the vision, risks, and action we have embarked on achieving. I have been guilty too often of expending large amounts of energy in unfocused activities, which resulted in marginal success.

When I narrowed my focus and exerted the same level of energy, I achieved much greater success. Think of releasing a balloon into a room. It will fly uncontrolled around the room and then dive to the floor devoid of energy. The same balloon released on a narrow track will speed down the path to a pre-determined destination before its power evaporates.

Our choice, chance, change, and channel are like the track above. They serve to maximize our efforts' energy and impact, resulting in a more substantial benefit for that profit from our production.

***

Fifth, we must make a **Commitment** to achieve our goal or dream. Our pledge requires a **dedication** to continuing the pursuit of our goal regardless of the obstacles. Most of us have launched ambitious efforts only to discard them after encountering resistance.

When we walk down the street focused on our destination, we fix our eyes on the finish line. It is easy to drop our focus to our feet if a pack of small dogs starts nipping at our ankles. Without an unwavering spirit, we cease to progress and abandon our quest.

Time has lost the name of the wise person who noted, "Dedication is the ability and determination to complete a resolution long after the mood in which it was made is gone." To accomplish our mission, we must progress relentlessly toward it.

***

Sixth, success only results from **Consistent** efforts. Similar to commitment, it is imperative to **persist** regularly despite distractions, perceived better opportunities, and setbacks. The larger the goal, the more energy is required to secure it.

People like Walt Disney, the Wright Brothers, Abraham Lincoln, and others are known for their achievements, but few know the length, breadth, and depth of their daily work to reach their pinnacles.

Early setbacks are a common thread amongst them and other of the greatest champions in life. They used the bitter taste of their shortfalls as motivation rather than accept defeat. Their examples show us our possibilities.

***

Seventh, we must **Come Again** over and over. Champions show up **every day** with their best effort. Many people slack off when the coach or boss isn't looking at them.

True champions always leave nothing on the field or workplace. They withstand others telling them they make them look bad and don't relax when no one is pushing them. They are self-motivated because they desire more than the team or business expects from them.

Champions set their targets of achievement, and pursue them all day, every day until accomplished. They then establish new and higher goals for themselves, knowing that they will not achieve their final mountaintop until life is complete.

***

Finally, when we exercise the seven C's above, we will stand as **Champions** on the mountain of success! It won't be easy, and the effort is not for the faint-hearted. Even if we don't achieve the highest peak, we will stand at a higher elevation than those timid souls who never departed from the life of comfort.

Hall-of-Fame and former coach at Oklahoma, Bud Wilkinson, who knew a lot about winning, said, "If you're going to be a champion, you must be willing to pay a greater price."

It all begins with our choice. When I have followed all of the steps and achieved national and international rewards and recognition, the accomplishment overshadows the worthwhile sacrifice and effort. It is a great feeling I hope everyone experiences.

***

What are the Seven Steps to Championship Performance in a Simple Formula?

Choice + Chance + Change + Channel + Commitment + Consistent + Come Again = Champion!

Or

Vision + Risk + Action + Focus + Dedication + Persistence + Every day = Champion!

***

We can do it! The question is, what dream do we have we're willing to pay the price to achieve?

IF HE CAN, WHY CAN'T WE?

The world can be a callous and unforgiving place. The voices of those who have fallen short that want to protect us from failure and others who would resent our achievements often speak louder than those of the people who desire our progress.

When things look bleak, it is beneficial to look to those who successfully endure challenges with optimism to lift our spirits. Their example shows us the only way we can attack our predicaments with any hope of overcoming them.

***

Too often, the media focuses on negativity and failure. When we find a positive and uplifting story, we need to absorb it for inspiration in our efforts.

I recently learned of Chris Koch in an uplifting article from *The Epoch Times*. He was born without arms or legs and grew up on his family farm in Canada. His parents did not treat him any differently than anyone else.

When he desired to play hockey, people helped him find a way to play. When he fell on the ice, they treated him like all of the other players.

Chris traveled to Ontario for part of his advanced studies and worked with a war amputation group. Later, he returned home to work in the airline industry before resuming his agricultural career.

Chris replaced prosthetic legs with a longboard and has completed several marathons. His long list of accomplishments includes hiking and sharing his remarkable story through public speaking.

His message should make us think and inspire us. He believes, **"If I can…."**

I admire Chris Koch and appreciate his inspirational example.

***

As I look back on my experiences, I see successes and setbacks. One component of the achievements was embarking on the objective with the confidence I could achieve it. Yes, I occasionally failed despite my spirit, but it was less often than other experiences. William James correctly observed, "It is our attitude at the beginning of a difficult task which, more than anything else, will affect its successful outcome."

When I review my shortcomings, whether it is a single golf shot or something more critical, I routinely see hesitancy or a lack of confidence in my ability.

***

Henry Ford stated, "There are those who think they can, and those who think they can't. They're both right." **The Only difference between can and can't is our Temperament.** If we believe we can't do something, we're defeated before we even begin. As my dad told me repeatedly, "Can't never did anything."

***

Another common threat to confidence in our abilities is a lack of persistence. Too often, we begin an enterprise with little faith and abandon it at the earliest failure. Chris Koch's success story in *The Epoch Times* didn't detail how many times he fell short before realizing his achievements, but we know it had to be numerous. Likewise, professional gymnast Jen Bricker, who was also born without legs, persisted relentlessly in every endeavor until she accomplished her goals.

It is almost unheard of that any successful people experience their ultimate performance levels on their initial attempts. If we dig beneath the accolades of their story, we will assuredly find untold hours of grueling work and repeated failures before consistent success.

President Calvin Coolidge artfully advises us, "**Nothing in this world can take the place of persistence.** Talent will not: nothing is more common than unsuccessful men with talent. Genius will not: unrewarded genius is almost a proverb. Education will not: the world is full of educated derelicts. Persistence and determination alone are omnipotent."

***

Another miracle of life is **that achievement builds confidence, leading to more success.** It is stunning what a lift an accomplishment can provide our attitudes regardless of its size. Additionally, increased assurance in our capabilities doesn't only occur in the area experienced but spills over into every other living space. Feeling good about our recent golf game can translate into fearlessness attacking other previously unachieved goals.

***

While success is our ultimate goal, there is no shame in not achieving it if we have exerted every ounce of energy in its attempt. John Wooden, who knew more than a little about success as a college basketball coach, taught, "*Success is peace of mind, which is a direct result of self-satisfaction in knowing you made the effort to become the best of which you are capable.*"

As a tool to achieve financial independence, I began investing in rental properties in the 1980s. Every year or two, I added a property to my portfolio. My plan, like that of so many other investors, seemed foolproof. Little did I know the lesson I was about to learn.

A change in federal tax law in 1986, made investing in rental real estate a poor choice. Investors fled the market resulting in a significant drop in values and making it difficult to sell properties.

My real estate investment adventure in the 1980s resulted in complete financial ruin after a two plus year fight for survival. My loss was substantial, but I learned a great deal that has benefitted me since then, and I have no regrets from my experience.

We will not live with the ultimate pain of regret when we always give our best effort in life.

***

How can we maximize our achievements and minimize our shortcomings?

1. We have to **begin believing we can achieve our objectives and dreams.**
2. As Chris Koch illustrates, "If I can…"
3. If we don't believe we can accomplish a feat, we've already lost.
4. "Can't never did anything." – Bill Battle.
5. We must **Persist** after reversals. Two adages still apply to life.
    *   Rome wasn't built in a day.
    *   If at first, you don't succeed, try, try, try again.
6. Every achievement builds our confidence, and increased confidence leads to more and more considerable successes.
7. If we pursue an endeavor with everything we have, we may not accomplish it, but we can rest knowing there was Nothing more we could have done.

***

The next time we face an intimidating obstacle, remembering Chris Koch's accomplishments, attitude, and example will fortify our resolve to triumph in the effort.

WHEN DID HUMOR DIE, AND
WHAT DO WE DO ABOUT IT?

When did humor die? Can we pinpoint a date, or were we subjected like the frog in the pot to a slowly increasing temperature until it was too late to survive?

***

If you don't remember or didn't notice the titanic shift in so-called comedy, I suggest you go onto www.youtube.com. Play clips from Johnny Carson, Bob Hope, Don Rickles, Rodney Dangerfield, Jay Leno, Lucille Ball, Flip Wilson, Phyllis Diller, Carol Burnett, and many others.

Watching those entertainers will transport you back to a time when vulgarity was not allowed on television, and the classiest and funniest comedians refrained from using it in their stage shows as well. You will find yourself laughing at jokes that often are as timely today as when they first aired.

Politicians from all political parties were equally ridiculed by comedians on both sides of the spectrum. Jokes were funny, while absent the foaming-at-the-mouth hatred we see too often today.

Today, so-called humorists find it essential to use coarse language in every sentence. Their political humor is one-sided, mean-spirited, and relentlessly used as a political tactic.

When did humor from time eternal die?

***

Unfortunately, we can't blame the murder of timeless humor solely on the comedians. A new, entitled, and never-to-be-offended generation has come of age, which insists the world accede to its every whim and throw away centuries of societal development. Politically correct only describes them in part. This new "audience" isn't satisfied with opting-out of entertainment they don't like but feel it a personal mission to eliminate anything they find offensive, and anyone who may wish to see or hear it be damned.

Jerry Seinfeld, who was so successful his last name became an entertainment icon, discontinued performing on college campuses in 2015 because the audiences were too politically correct. They not only didn't laugh at anything but attributed every joke offered as "sexist, racist, homophobic, etc."

I look for and find humor in almost every situation in life. It is healthier and more fun to laugh than to always find fault and be angry. We used to laugh at ourselves and use self-deprecating humor to endear ourselves to others. I have poked fun at people and been made fun of by an uncountable number of people.

When did we become too sensitive to laugh and laugh at ourselves?

***

Children naturally enjoy laughter and learn to tell jokes soon after they discover how to speak. How many knock-knock jokes have you heard from children? How many times has someone asked, "Why did the chicken cross the road?"

If things proceed on the current trajectory, the next generation of children will have their humor suppressed before their first kindergarten day. Their parents belong to today's soulless and humorless class. They won't dare want their little darlings offending knocks, chickens, or any other recipient of their children's zest for life.

How many generations will suffer before political correctness is vanquished?

***

Someone whose name has been lost in time first stated, "Laughter is the best medicine!" How correct they were, and how much more satisfying is life when we can freely laugh at the daily occurrences we experience. We accept the fact it takes fewer muscles to smile than frown. Similarly, I would rather have laugh lines than frown lines on my face!

We have the freedom to choose the humor we desire for our entertainment. Others are free to choose their form of humor. It is not my right to "cancel" entertainment they like any more than it is it is their right to "cancel" the programming I choose.

I believe the exception is our exercise of self-restraint in exposing children to adult-oriented material. Content standards have evaporated during my lifetime to the detriment of our society, all in the name of allowing the presenter unfettered free speech. It reveals when a person who insisted on creative freedom to expose other children to adult material finally realizes their impact. They plead for others not to illuminate their children with similar content.

When will the pendulum swing back in balancing individual rights with protecting children?

***

We have been blessed by our forefathers with the First Amendment to the U.S. Constitution, guaranteeing our freedom of speech. My parents taught me the adage, "sticks and stones may break my bones, but words shall never hurt me." If someone said something ugly to me, my parents told me to let it roll off my shoulders, buck up, and go forward with my life.

While we should be free to exercise and enjoy our freedom to speak, we must also realize comments others make may say something we disagree with in claiming their rights.

When will we restore the proper balance between speaking freely and refraining from speaking freely out of respect for others?

What Can We Do Today to Restore Laughter to our Daily Lives?

1. Stand up and reclaim your First Amendment right to Free Speech!
2. Look for the humor in everything in life! You'll be surprised how often you find it!
3. Laughter is the best medicine. It is the only medicine acceptable to become addicted to in life.
4. Laughter is calorie-free. Apply it to your life early and often each day.
5. Laughter is always in season.
6. Except for the angry crowd, laughter never goes out of style.
7. Accept others' humor you may disagree with to preserve your freedom for comedy of our choice.
8. Encourage children and others to laugh and find humor in life at every opportunity.
9. Oppose and defeat political correctness and its soul-stealing suffocation always.

We are blessed to live at a beautiful time in history. We have more time and choices for leisure activities than any previous generation. Life is excellent, and we should be free to enjoy it fully with as much and the type of laughter of our choosing.

Is There Any Place
We Can Escape Politics?

Will we ever return to a day when politics doesn't infect every area of our lives?

I'm grateful to have lived when there were sacred refuges from political discussions. We could go to church or movie theaters, watch entertainment on television, and do sports for their enjoyment alone. It permitted us a "sanctuary" to escape the severe matters of life.

***

I love sports and used to love professional sports. Today, the constant injection of politics by athletes, media, team leaders, and league officials has relegated me to supporting golf and rodeo. Millions of others join me. Whether we support a person, party, or issue, or not, we want politics out of sports, period.

***

Yes, injustices in life have, are, and will happen regardless of our form of government because of flaws in the human heart. We can all improve our views and the treatment of others.

Our country was founded on noble ideals but implemented erratically due to man's imperfections. History records our successes and failures as we strive to "form a more perfect union."

Perfect attainment of our ideals is impossible, but the effort is worthwhile. The result to date is the freest, fairest, and most prosperous country in world history.

***

Political statements in professional sports took a dramatic uptick in 2016 when a player sat for *The Star-Spangled Banner*. When asked about his action later, he stated he would not show pride in the flag of a country that oppressed people of color.

Another player advised the initial instigator to kneel instead of sit for the anthem, which he did and was quickly emulated by others.

For some time, media and others confused the public, reporting the demonstration was not against the flag and what it represented.

Subsequent events and time have only reinforced that player's and others' hatred for our flag and country.

***

I don't mind players standing, sitting, kneeling, or lying on the field. They can do it before, during, or after the game.

My prejudice is liking players who enter the field, assemble in the end-zone before the game, kneel, and say a quiet prayer. I'm sure some people are insulted by that action.

The issue then is one of timing. Why do some feel the only time to kneel in protest of our country is during the playing of our national anthem?

How stupid do they think we are when they mask their actions saying they don't disrespect the men and women who have served, fought, and died for that flag and our country? It also insults all past, present, and future citizens who love our country.

It is ALL about their hatred for our country and the flag and anthem that celebrate it.

Watching and listening to the kneelers' other actions confirms their bitterness for the country, enabling their wealth by playing a child's game.

***

Why should those who feel as I continue to spend our hard-earned dollars and time supporting people who insist on subjecting us to political statements during a game, television show, movie, or other performance?

Is there anything we can do to return our beloved sports, movies, television programs, and other pastimes to pure entertainment without constant political messages?

***

What Can We Do?
1. **Vote with your dollars – Find activities that haven't succumbed to political correctness and activism.**
2. **Vote with your feet – If you find yourself at an event that turns into a political rally or demonstration, get up and leave.**
3. **Vote with your voice – Let leagues, teams, and advertisers hear from you.**

Hollywood survived a scandal in the 1950s where perceived communists and communist sympathizers could not work because they were blacklisted. France recovered from The Reign of Terror in the 1790s. The *Bible* tells us, This, too, shall come to pass.

My hope is this period passes quickly, and we can return to a period where sports and entertainment receive rewards based on their merit.

When the public demands that time, it will return.

I'm casting my votes now and appreciate your consideration of doing likewise.

***

May God bless America!

Welcome to Jungle Life
2022 Style

The Law of the Jungle is defined as "survival of the fittest" or "anything goes" by Wikipedia.

If some politicians obtain what they're demanding, the thin blue lines of law enforcement will be neutered or worse. The result will deliver us into a jungle not seen in our country since settlers first landed on our shores.

***

Protests and riots in our streets result from years of education, media, and other institutions teaching our people to hate their country and its founding.

Absent is gratitude for the founders who gave us something better than we had and anyone else has today.

Also missing is an appreciation for the men and women who have fought and sometimes given their "last full measure," as President Lincoln described during his Gettysburg Address. Their sacrifice has sustained our individual liberty and economic freedom.

***

The real haters in our country want to destroy our unique gift as citizens in exchange for a promised utopia of equality and security, resulting in our loss of individual liberty and the pursuit of happiness.

Their ignorance or refusal to acknowledge every previous implementation of this utopian promise has resulted in misery, tyranny, slavery to the government, and millions of deaths.

The ignorance of those advocating the sacrifice of freedom for socialism is only exceeded by their arrogance. Advocates believe, like those who preceded them, it will work this time because they will be in charge and are more intelligent than those who previously failed. Leading from behind, they will create a jungle atmosphere for the masses to prepare them for the promised utopia.

***

For the people, every day becomes one of survival. It will be similar to the game show, but everyone is a contestant and is playing for keeps instead of a material prize.

People will have no perspective of the past that Adversaries erased to discard the success of Western civilization.

They will have no purpose in life other than serving the government because opponents removed God from public discussion and worship.

Individuals will not plan for the future because government organizers disdain personal growth and striving to succeed.

The result will be a monotonous life where people experience equal misery every day with no hope of escape. Equality of suffering, in reality, will be much harsher than equality of "the people" promised with freedom's sacrifice.

***

This paints a bleak picture for sure, but never one to discontinue our efforts to return to "life, liberty, and the pursuit of happiness," as stated in the Declaration of Independence in 1776.

There is a road back to purpose, peace, prosperity, planning, and personal growth that our forefathers wrote if we're bold enough to choose it. It will not be easy nor without pain and sacrifice, but our forefathers paid the price once, and we can do so once again for our children and descendants.

***

What Can We Do Today to Reclaim our Life, Liberty, and Pursuit of Happiness?

1. Seek and return God into our lives and the public square.
2. Re-adopt the values and ethics of Western civilization.
3. Elevate standards and expectations of individuals and leaders to inspire personal growth.
4. Reinstitute limited power, separation of power, and checks and balances in our governmental bodies.
5. Remember and revere the past sacrifice of our forefathers.
6. Recognize our blessings and publicly proclaim them so we never forget our privileges.
7. Resume teaching the exceptionalism and uniqueness of The United States in our schools to instill pride into our future generations.

We are blessed to live at this time and allowed to extend the freedom we provided to unborn citizens in the future. As former Texas Attorney General and Secretary of State John Ben Shepperd said, **"To be born free is an accident, to live free is a responsibility, but to die free is an obligation."**

The spotlight is on us. Will we stand up to the threat? Or will we doom those in the future to a less-rewarding life than we were gifted?

PREVARICATORS DEFENDING THE INDEFENSIBLE

Dictionary.com defines a prevaricator as someone who speaks falsely or is a liar. Avoiding the truth is so commonly displayed today, someone probably wrote a book that compliments their savvy counsel to those caught in an untruth in an emergency.

When someone is exposed and does not possess the truth, how do they respond? The honorable response is to admit guilt, ask for mercy, and repent of the offense.

Here, we'll review the importance of always telling the truth and explore how people react when caught in mistruths.

***

In the quaint old times that built our civilization, truth mattered above all else. It was paramount to human relations. People transacted business by a handshake and one's word of honor. Failure to keep one's commitment branded the transgressor a liar and worse.

Being a truthful person is a subset of being dependable and honorable. Honor meant everything to people because everyone needed family, friends, and neighbors to assist them when the chips were down. Helping others in need cemented your reputation and made them ready to reciprocate for you. There are people I would trust with my daughter's life, and I hope to have earned a similar place in their hearts. I wonder if honor isn't as crucial today because people believe the government will permanently save them and having trusted friends isn't as important?

***

Without truth and honor, there is no trust, and without faith, civilization decays into a dog-eat-dog jungle existence.

Many faiths teach the importance of truthfulness, and governing bodies based on faith value facts. Any society where the people and their representatives honor and live truthfully is preferable to any institution where each individual relatively defines truth.

Courtroom oaths ask witnesses to swear to "tell the truth, the whole truth, and nothing but the truth so help you, God." At one time, the fear of exposure as a perjurer compelled most people to honor that vow. Today, I believe many are unafraid of being caught in a lie or suffering any penalty upon discovery. The last time I testified in court the "so help you God" portion was absent from the oath, elevating people's confidence in fibbing. I believe there is still something in those words for everyone but the most hardened atheists. Who wants to take a chance breaking an oath to God?

Native Americans highly valued truthfulness and honor and described those who didn't tell the truth as "two-faced" or speaking with a "forked-tongue." They held people who communicated the straight, unvarnished truth in high esteem like any other society.

Saul Alinsky spent a lifetime "organizing" revolution utilizing and Americanizing Marxist tactics. In his manifesto, *Rules for Radicals*, he unmoored radicals from the truth as a tactic of moral relativism to attain success. He advocated telling enemies what they wanted to hear while doing what you wanted to do. That elixir has and is still being used to dupe people into voting and acting in ways to abandon their current lifestyle for a promised utopia.

***

My dad taught me, "the biggest lie in the world is a half-truth." How wise that statement is because the boldest lies are always clothed in small pieces of the truth to enhance their deceit.

While not limited to politicians, they seemed to have better perfected the tactics below when they're desperately trying to avoid wearing the tag of a liar. Public relations professionals earn excellent incomes advising people how to communicate and respond to attain their objectives.

When people who employ misrepresentations don't possess the truth, they implement these seven defenses to dodge guilt:

1. They **DENY** the act or statement in its entirety. Part of their efforts **DISAVOW** and or **DISCLAIM** the charges against them. They hope their bold, loud, and repeated defense will **DISCOURAGE** those pursuing them.

2. They **DEFLECT** the accusation by focusing on another topic. In everyday language, they **DIVERT** attention. What you're accusing me of is unimportant while we have much more critical issues to focus on today.

3. They **DISTRACT** their accusers through various techniques designed to throw them off of the trail to the truth. They fire everything but the kitchen sink at those questioning their action to **DISORIENT, DISCOMBOBULATE, DAZE, DISARRANGE,** and **DISORDER** information. These tactics make their **DECEIT** trail more challenging to follow and bring them to justice.

4. They **DECEIVE** the public repeatedly with a straight face. Only a select number of people can do this, making them too dangerous to entrust to public office or any position of responsibility. They're masters who **DUPE, DEFRAUD,** and **DELUDE** people without conscious thought.

5. They **DEMORALIZE** their prosecutors because they always appear to win and escape punishment until the very moment of their fall.

6. They **DAMAGE** everyone who stands between them and getting their way. Desperate people commit daring

actions to cover their wrongdoing. It is nothing to **DEFACE** or **DISMANTLE** their opposition to win at all costs.

7. They **DESTROY completely** anyone who has survived the first six defenses. They say a cornered wounded animal is the most dangerous of all animals. A human who has failed to cover their untruths with the six previous techniques will **DESTROY** their enemies without remorse or regret. When facing someone in this position, it is imperative to utilize all means to defend ourselves and the truth until ultimate victory.

***

Our best defense against those who distort the truth for personal gain is swift and painful prosecution of their misdeeds. The pain of the punishment must exceed the achievement of the action significantly to dissuade further offense and, as an example, deter others in the future.

Human nature, what it is, will consistently deliver those who will chance a lie for advancement. Our only hope is the discouragement from discipline will contain those numbers below our modern experiences.

DREAM AND DARE!

Some people advocate we dare to dream in life, but dreaming alone requires no action. I propose we dream and dare to achieve our hopes through our performance.

Thunder without lightning is nothing, and it is the same as dreams without daring action to accomplish them.

Many dreams languish as merely thoughts due to the uncertainty faced by those who may pursue them. Other goals are discarded upon the path to their attainment at mile-markers, noting where the various obstacles destroyed them.

Despite our most fervent desires and efforts, when we act, no one can eliminate the risks of life in the quest to achieve our dreams.

**

Our first requirement for attaining our dreams is to adopt a **positive attitude** and eliminate debilitating negative thoughts. Yes, caution is prudent. Yes, considering risks and preparing contingencies for setbacks along the way are beneficial. Prior failures are common for nearly everyone who has achieved noteworthy success.

However, we cannot allow the possibility of defeat or difficulty to destroy the belief in our dream.

No dream is too big to pursue!

We're never Too Young, Too Old, or Too Late to seek our dreams!

If you have postponed your dreams, do not despair because "a dream delayed is not a dream denied."

If you fail to achieve your dreams, do not lament because realizing a shortfall in your attempt is better than the lifelong sorrow of regret.

Henry Ford said, "There are those who think they can, and those who think they can't. They're both right." Each of us is free to choose which side of Ford's statement we occupy. Our choice bears a disproportionate weight in the results of all of our efforts.

Walt Disney, Thomas Edison, Helen Keller, Colonel Harland Sanders, Martin Luther King Jr., and many other worldwide successes began their journeys positively and overcame countless challenges and setbacks.

***

Positioning ourselves to launch the effort to achieve a dream is extremely important. It includes making many minute decisions that aren't important on the surface, but in aggregate, build positive and avoid negative preparation.

When our vision appears, or we determine it is time to embark on its pursuit, we will increase our odds of success if we remember the 7 P's. I learned of them many years ago in the Jaycees. They have served me well since then. They are **Proper Prior Planning Prevents Pitifully Poor Performances.**

Benjamin Disraeli advised, "The secret of success in life is to be ready when your opportunity comes." Noted racecar driver Bobby Unser added, "Success is when preparation and opportunity meet."

We never know when we will visualize our dreams. If we have adequately prepared, we can begin our adventure immediately.

***

Until we **step forward in action**, victory is impossible regardless of our attitude, positioning, and preparation.

I'm an average golfer on my very best day. A friend taught me the importance of commitment to your swing in golf, and it is incredible the difference it makes. When I swing with fear, uncertainty, or doubt in my mind, the result is invariably awful. On the other hand, when I commit to my swing and execute it expecting success, the ball responds to my commitment.

The same dedication and commitment are necessary for success in every enterprise in life. Dorothea Brande implores us to "Act as if it were impossible to fail." Her warning was present in my every success and absent in every loss.

***

Too many people today believe we should not experience consequences for poor decisions and life's vagaries. They live in a fantasy world with the hope of enduring but not suffering any loss. What a wonderful world it would be if that were real?

The COVID-19 pandemic in 2020 was unforeseen, unanticipated, and unavoidable for most of us. It appeared out of the blue, which is when most catastrophic events occur.

Individual actions limited the risk of infection, but pre-pandemic decisions preset financial, emotional, psychological, and other parameters completing each individual's experience of the event.

While some retreated into their homes and awaited government officials to signal the all-clear to emerge and discover the carnage, others made different choices.

Like our ancestors and others who experienced unexpected and uncontrollable changes in their lives, people driven to accomplish dreams, goals, and objectives responded differently. They picked themselves up off of the floor, shook off any short-term self-pity, and adjusted to the new reality. They triumphantly responded to Mike Tyson's challenge, "Everybody has a plan until they get punched in the face."

***

Dreamers who succeed change tactics, recommit themselves, and resume their course undaunted by any diversion. When COVID-19 is long gone, we'll look back and tell their stories. We can hope our victories will be among them!

***

How can we maximize the possibility of achieving our life's dreams?

1. A **Positive Attitude** is necessary before we expend any energy chasing a dream.
2. Strive in every decision, large and small in life, to **Position** yourself ready to attempt any dream that appears in your future.
3. **Preparation using the 7 P's** and planning our journey will make the trip smoother.
4. No dream or plan is possible unless we **Commit** and **ACT!** Despite our wishes and desires, we will make mistakes.
5. **Anticipate** the consequences of incorrect decisions, unexpected events, and any unrelated development you can imagine that threatens your success.
6. **Change tactics** as quickly as possible to protect your strategic objectives.
7. **Celebrate your victory**, visualize your next dream, and repeat!

***

Dreams are marvelous but worthless unless we Dare to pursue them!

May you boldly envision your dreams, dare greatly, commit your efforts, touch untold numbers of people, and enjoy many victories!

Successfully Navigating Change in the Post-COVID World

The Five Skills Essential to Lead Your Team to Victory

The Industrial Revolution ushered into the world a paradigm shift in technology unseen previously and ever-increasing in speed since. United States citizens seized and continue to grasp opportunities quicker than other countries because of the twin freedoms of individual political independence and economic liberty.

Over time, the appearance and substance of change became more predictable and easier to factor into business planning.

Then, like the tsunami of the Industrial Revolution, COVID-19 introduced change utterly different from previously experienced when it appeared with little public warning in March 2020.

***

Organizations responded on the fly with the advent of COVID installing temporary policies and procedures, intending to eliminate them when things returned to "normal."

Two years plus into the COVID world, case levels, hospitalizations, and deaths have subsided somewhat, but signs of a pre-COVID normal are absent.

Some of the revisions installed temporarily will be challenging to unwind because people like them. Working from home agrees with some people. Others are thrilled to choose nontraditional work hours. Converting temporary modifications into permanent processes confirms the return to the previous normal is unattainable. Ralph Waldo Emerson's statement, **"The mind, once stretched by a new idea, never returns to its original dimensions,"** may have envisioned a time such as this.

I believe the workplace and interpersonal teams will not be the same as the pre-COVID world in our lifetimes. While fruitful, temporary changes will need renewed appraisals to ensure their superior effectiveness for the new normal.

With the same can-do spirit of their forefathers who overcame wars, depressions, and previous pandemics, Americans will adapt and flourish in the future. Our most significant threat is misdirected government strangling the goose that laid the golden egg of prosperity with soul-stifling taxes, rules, and social engineering.

Human souls yearn to improve life for themselves and their families. Each of us is created uniquely with different gifts. Adam Smith recognized this long ago when he said, "Individual Ambition Serves the Common Good." There are many skills I lack and pay those gifted with them to provide me. Likewise, I have a few skills others don't, and they pay me to deliver them for their benefit. The free exchange of our work utilizing our gifts with others is the basis for the free-market economy.

This free exchange of labor is necessary for economic progress, technological innovation, and improving living standards. Unfortunately, it disturbs those who want equity, sameness, and control. Some Americans display an interest in a controlled economy until they discover it strangles the human spirit. Like Las Vegas gamblers, they would rather have a messy economy with freedom and opportunity than no opportunity for improving their futures.

***

So, how do we lead our teams to organization and individual success in a new normal?

We must take **five steps** to ensure **our RAPID response to change leads to sustainable success.**

***

First, those who **Recognize change is inevitable** will position themselves to execute the other four steps and succeed. Innovation seems obvious, but it is incredible how many people painfully experience a difference after it occurs because they were surprised.

We rarely can control the timing of changes, but becoming a student prepares us for its appearance. The hi-tech world is a beautiful example as we are constantly presented with new products with game-changing capabilities before their predecessors have exhausted their service.

Companies adeptly obscure their development efforts, which results in jaw-dropping product introductions with little or no warning. Early adopters to change pioneer new inventions proving their value and influencing the masses to follow in their acceptance.

***

Second, successful leaders **Anticipate challenges** and visualize their appearance, responses, and ensuing results.

Long before COVID, businesses dealt with remote employees, but nontraditional work-at-home employees reacted in various ways to their forced time away from the office.

Some need the bonding with fellow employees like a sales rep I inherited in Denver. He couldn't function well without going to an office and spending time with his teammates before departing for his calls.

Others will cherish working at home, some successfully and others not so much. Management has to supervise each one individually, utilizing one set of rules. Too loose oversight reduces production, and micromanagement drives employees away. Interpersonal skills are a premium for leadership.

A third group will thrive in a hybrid environment working in the office part of the time and from home the remainder. Again, this new option tests management more than a traditional office operation.

Employee and management reviews and surveys require revision to reveal traits leading to each team member's maximum success and fulfillment.

***

Third, the best leaders, over time, **Plan several alternative responses**, which cover a wide range of possible events. Solid planning minimizes surprises like football teams see when opponents change their offensive or defensive schemes before a game.

Strong organizations will thoroughly review policies and procedures, codifying changes made during the pandemic that enhance long-term success. These include new rules for working from home, the office, or hybrid work schedules.

Like any human endeavor, one-size leadership doesn't fit all people. When we expect more from people and help them maximize their potential, they will deliver more for the entire organization.

The 7 P's of Proper Prior Planning Prevents Pitifully Poor Performance will help us optimally control what we can control.

***

Fourth, **Identify change's arrival as soon as possible!** Observant leaders endowed with the first three skills will notice different circumstances and issues earlier than less skillful managers.

Early recognition enables people to respond calmly with positive attitudes, which increases organization morale. It also instills confidence the leader will overcome whatever event has occurred.

Prior preparation allows calm deliberation of alternatives, and the vital consideration **example** and **precedent** will establish for the future. I can't emphasize enough the importance of considering **precedent** and **example** in any decision. Failure to adequately do so can necessitate frequent management rulings to correct short-sightedness and increase stability.

People and events will test our leadership skills, especially during the most trying times. Promoted to lead former peers years ago, one team member distrusted my ability despite his friendly demeanor. Rightfully, he withheld his respect until I demonstrated I deserved to lead the team.

Once earned, that gentleman and I became best of friends, and he eventually led the entire sales organization of that firm.

***

Finally, champions don't wait for perfect information, but decisively **Dash to act** with enough intelligence to make informed decisions.

As George Foreman says, "Everyone has a plan until they get punched in the face." Expect portions of plans to fail. Adapt to new data, adjust and change the project in real-time to ensure success and avert failure.

Unlike theory, challenges in the real world are asymmetrical and messy. Many people are apprehensive of new realities and cautious about changing processes institutionalized over several years.

Flexible leaders effectively overcome short-term challenges with minimal adverse long-term effects on their organizations.

Despite changing environments, solid leaders build and adjust organizations for long-term success. It is said people quit managers and not companies. Conversely, successful leaders are prized and attract the best talent to join their team and achieve maximum fulfillment.

***

Whether change appears often and quickly or slowly and rarely. Whether it results from COVID-19 or other unexpected sources, good leaders will face and expertly overcome it because they instinctively implement these five steps:
- **Recognize change is inevitable.**
- **Anticipate challenges** and visualize their appearance, responses, and ensuing results.

- **Plan several alternative responses,**
- **Identify change's arrival as soon as possible!**
- Decisively **Dash to act.**

Thankfulness Should Be an Everyday American Attitude

While Thanksgiving is an annual celebration of a thankful heart and a way to honor the Pilgrims, if we adopt a thankful attitude every day, our lives will be happier, more successful, and better examples for our descendants.

***

For most of our history, the struggle to live and provide a better life for one's descendants demanded almost everyone's constant attention. There was no time for leisure, frivolity, and self-focus through pandemics, depression, war, economic cycles, or individual and family issues.

Our ancestors were serious people because it was required to survive. Their combined efforts built the most prosperous country in the history of the world. With success came leisure time and idle hours produced self-focus resulting in celebrating narcissism culminating in frivolous "look-at-me" exhibitionism.

To see the degradation of our culture, one must merely review movies from the 1930s through the 1950s. The language utilized was broader, more civilized, and targeted to elevate the minds of the audience. People rarely used profanity as they effectively communicated emotions without it. Plots were more intricate and touched a full range of human emotions. Everyone dressed more formally, and the sets displayed an elegance affirming a thriving society.

Citizens recognized the source of their bounties and appreciated them because they and the country had survived mortal threats. They knew life did not guarantee liberty, health, and prosperity.

Rather than cement an ever-improving civilization, new generations moved farther away from the experience of the 1918 Spanish Flu, the Great Depression of the 1930s, and World War I and II. Temporary threats in Korea and Vietnam did not appear to threaten the American way of life. The War on Terror is sold to the public as a temporary inconvenience to Western civilization.

A permanent entitlement of success permeated the country, and privilege and thankfulness devolved into expectation and demands. Instead of people appreciating what they had, attention focused on what was missing.

***

American pop culture and the general media promote our unhappiness with life. Their cumulative message for people is to focus on: **Self, Today only, Materialism, Instant gratification, What we don't have, and the Fame of personality vs. achievement,** accomplishes what any adversary desires. That is a defeatist attitude.

Anyone subscribing to the pop culture and media messages will most likely:
- **envy others they believe live better lives**
- **feel dissatisfaction in where their lives are**
- **experience discouragement from pursuing their dreams**
- **focus on "why me" when adversity strikes**
- **see everything in a negative or glass-half-empty attitude**

***

Our human nature more readily adopts negative messages than positive ones. Have you ever noticed the bustling motivation industry where speakers and authors live to lift people's spirits, but there isn't one looking at life negatively? It affirms the natural state and ease of adopting negative thoughts as standard practice.

Eric Hoffer said, "The hardest arithmetic to master is that which enables us to count our blessings." It is so profound because it is a continual struggle to overcome life's daily challenges and demons. Once we stray onto a trail of negativism, it takes a proactive approach to reverse course and resume our positive attitude and efforts.

A life unsaved from a pessimistic viewpoint will be unproductive and unhappy. As I have previously said, you can't accomplish anything positive with a negative attitude.

***

When we focus on Positives/Blessings, we will be happier and more likely to realize our dreams. President Theodore Roosevelt said, "Believe you can, and you're halfway there."

Thankfulness is a way of daily life. I've observed common elements in those who are happy in life. They radiate many of the following characteristics worthy of adoption for we who desire peace and contentment. See if you agree with my conclusion.

People who are more often happy in life are those who focus on:

- Faith in their Creator
- Others instead of themselves
- Lifetime and beyond impact from their actions
- Spiritual significance and relationships instead of materialism
- Deferred gratification
  - The only thing we should compare ourselves to is where we were yesterday.
- Celebrating what they have
  - Johnson Oatman Jr.'s hymn, "Count Your Blessings," is a source of encouragement.
- Concentrate on achievement, and trust earned rewards will occur.

- Equal opportunities enable people to employ their individual gifts.
- Everyone contributing their gifts results in a synergy greater than the sum of the parts.
  o   2 + 2 = 5
- Asking "what now" when adversity strikes
- Seeing life with a positive glass-half-full attitude.

***

We Americans have more to be thankful for than any people in history. The individual liberty bestowed upon us by our founders could have occurred only with divine intervention. The ideals established were unique in history and beneficial to all when executed faithfully. We can trace our shortcomings to the imperfections of humanity, which illustrates the founders' brilliance in instituting checks and balances and limiting power so no one or group could abuse power to harm the people.

We should be thankful for the existence of the instruments to return vigilant adherence to the founding principles and documents.

***

My last illustration is a personal one. Kent Greene and I were friends for 28 years and worked together for many of them. During the spring of 2018, we were both fighting cancer. My prognosis and result were more positive than his.

For the last several months of his life, we spoke almost daily. I ventured to New Orleans and spent three days sharing our faith and friendship before the ravages of stage 4 pancreatic cancer overwhelmed him.

While I labored to encourage him and lift his spirits, I found he lifted mine more. He encouraged my endeavor to communicate my experience through *Unwelcome Opportunity: Overcoming Life's Greatest Challenges*. I had forwarded him the manuscript for his benefit and comment.

Recognizing he wouldn't have the luxury of writing his story, I was one of two friends to encourage him to video his message of faith to those who were fortunate enough to find it after his departure.

I cannot encourage you enough to go to YouTube and watch *Amazing Joy Before Death* at the following link: https:// youtu.be/Qzy_Wd7jcQk. He closed with a message each of us should remember daily. "A happy heart is a thankful heart, and a thankful heart is a happy heart."

Kent Greene passed away on October 18, 2018. I miss him often and look forward to a future reunion.

ACHIEVERS SUNG AND UNSUNG ARE
THE REAL HEROES TO CELEBRATE

For more than 200 years, millions of Americans have worked diligently, seeking their dreams, providing for their families, and contributing to the development of the most prosperous country in the history of the world. We feel entitled to things our parents could only dream about, and our grandparents could not conceive.

Most people generally pursue happiness, envisioning ever-improving lives and gifting their children better futures.

***

For many years, the absence of leisure time and technology constrained the elevation of all but a very few to celebrity status. Statesmen, military heroes, explorers, and occasional authors or performers found themselves in the public spotlight.

Examples include George Washington, Abraham Lincoln, Dwight Eisenhower, Douglas MacArthur, Theodore Roosevelt, Merriweather Lewis and William Clark, Charles Lindbergh, Amelia Earhart, Clara Barton, Emily Dickinson, Helen Keller, Martin Luther King Jr., Harriet Tubman, The Wright Brothers, and Laura Ingalls Wilder are but a minuscule fraction of ordinary Americans who earned recognition for extraordinary achievements.

The common denominator among them and others I could have added were they completed impressive accomplishments before receiving recognition. None of them are perfect or are we.

The public honored their triumphs and overlooked or forgave their shortcomings.

For the most part, they each retained their humility and continued working and contributing to their families and country throughout their lives.

***

The real heroes building our great country are the nameless and faceless soldiers, law enforcement officers, doctors, nurses, farmers and ranchers, truckers, energy workers, restaurants, municipal workers, teachers, builders and construction workers, health care providers, financial institutions, and other categories more numerous than I can list here.

More likely than not, we will come into this world, live and work in our chosen field, and exit with little recognition or appreciation. However, everyone who labors in a legitimate arena contributes to our shared success and is worthy of gratitude and respect.

Adam Smith advocated in *The Wealth of Nations* in 1776 in free societies where people could pursue their chosen commerce, there was an invisible hand at work, which benefitted everyone. His quote, "Individual Ambition Serves the Common Good," is best validated by the long-term expanding prosperity achieved by the United States.

***

Fast-forward to the present, and we find countless numbers of individuals elbowing each other, grasping for an advantage to achieve fame.

Influencers and reality "stars" appear overnight celebrated by pop culture because of the number of clicks they receive on social media. Their fundamental contributions beyond themselves are challenging to identify, yet they bask in the glow of a public subset satisfied with superficial achievements.

The majority of heroes portrayed in entertainment are fictional or cartoon characters, and they are impervious to contemporary society's human imperfections. The failure to tell the stories of real American heroes is a disservice to present and future citizens. If we instead return to a comprehensive picture of an individual's performance, they can serve as inspirational beacons enabling other citizens to reach higher performance levels and enrich everyone's lives.

Athletes and entertainers receive more excessive adulation than at any time in our history. Previous generations witnessed ballplayers and movie stars sacrifice years off their careers and lives, volunteering to serve in World War II as an example. When the War on Terror escalated after 9/11, you could count on one hand their counterparts who left the field or theater for service. Arizona Cardinals football star Pat Tillman was a notable exception who paid the ultimate price serving his country.

The common thread among these groups is how disconnected they are from the public compared to their predecessors. Despite the distance from their bubble to their fellow citizens, many are eager to speak in the public square advocating policies often different from those held by the ordinary, unsung heroes who make the country flourish day in and day out.

***

We are blessed to live in a country with individual political and economic freedom, and our independence enables us to pursue whatever path we choose whenever we choose it. Whether we scale grand heights and achieve monumental victories, or labor unobserved by the majority, we are all critical to the present and future for ourselves, our families, and our country.

We were gifted this liberty by our innumerable forebears, who each added their touch to the reality we experience. Yes, we should enjoy life. But we also are responsible for honoring past generations on whose shoulders we stand and pass along an equal or more significant gift to future generations by broadening our shoulders to provide them a steady footing.

***

If we properly praise, thank, and encourage all who make our lives better each day, we will reap richer lives. And, if we only applaud actual achievement instead of fame, maybe pop culture will shift away from celebrating fame and honor exceptional accomplishments.

OUR TRADITIONS AND CULTURE ARE
THE GLUE HOLDING US TOGETHER

The self-righteous hellbent on a mission to devoid our culture of past imperfections intentionally or not is inflicting generational destruction challenging to repair. Their ingratitude for the modern conveniences of 21st century American life and focus on the shortcomings of past and present contributors to our society is breathtaking.

One by one, they destroy someone or something exceptional that citizens who love their country celebrate. The result is a culture ever descending into sameness with every other nation.

Our education system abandoned its role of instructing students on the uniqueness of our founding, development, ascension to world power status, and a beacon of hope throughout the world for those yearning for a land to live freely.

Let's remember a few examples of American greatness focusing on the positive results and leaving the negative focus on others to trumpet.

***

Many believe the hand of providence assembled the men and women who founded the United States. Their dissatisfaction with their government did not demand a cultural change but one of its power distribution and representation.

Instead of emotionally venting their frustrations and rashly reacting in an unorganized manner resulting in failure, they examined previous governmental structures selecting excellent characteristics and avoiding those that caused the societal collapse.

Their basic premises based on a consistency of human nature from the beginning of man directed them to construct a representative republic placing the most power with individual citizens, the second most power with the states who created the federal government, and the least power enumerated and limited to it. They feared the power of a monarch and head of a national power.

***

July 4th, 1776, the American **Declaration of Independence** was signed and declared. Representatives stated grievances formalizing the revolution unlike any other in history.

After seven long years of war with the sacrifice of so many, the citizens secured independence. The **Articles of Confederation** was the initial national government formed by the states. It failed because states reserved too much power for themselves, resulting in state militias, money, courts, an impotent Congress, and no executive branch to balance the legislature.

In 1787, delegates gathered in Philadelphia to improve the Articles and instead created an entirely new **Constitution.** Its success is evident by its being the longest-serving government instrument in history. It implemented a bicameral legislature with one house representing heavily populated states and the second to protect the sparsely populated states. It added an executive branch elected nationally and a judicial branch appointed by the executive brilliantly separated and limited power from any person or group.

The plan was so extraordinary that Benjamin Franklin replying to a lady who asked what type of government they created, said, "A republic if you can keep it." He knew the difficulty of restraining people from abusing their power, which even children can recognize today.

While the Constitution established individual rights, many feel the **Bill of Rights,** the most spectacular portion of the plan, was added in 1791. It recognized that people's rights come from God and are immutable. As Thomas Jefferson advised, "A government big enough to give you everything you need is big enough to take everything you have." We must remember any right conferred by people can just as quickly be revoked by other people, and the precedent can lead to a life with no individual rights.

The codification of free speech, the freedoms of religion, assembly, petitioning the government of grievances, the right to bear arms, protection of private property, and the stated restriction limiting the federal government to the very few enumerated responsibilities are some of the original ten amendments to the Constitution.

***

Other exceptional aspects of our country promote unity, national pride, cultural promotion, and individual industry.

In 1782, Congress added the motto, **"E. Pluribus Unum,"** meaning, "Out of many, one" to the Great Seal of the United States and many coins over the years. It states the essentialness of national success that regardless of where people come from to The United States, they should assimilate into the American culture and swear allegiance only to America. Today we see many immigrants retain all of their homeland's culture and accept none from their adopted country. Others hold multiple citizenships, which I don't believe benefits any country.

In God, We Trust is now the official motto of the United States, replacing E. Pluribus Unum in 1956. While I believe it superior to its predecessor, I like both. Faithful people arrived early on our shores, and religious worship is still an essential piece of our culture.

Equal justice under the law is another premise ideal in theory but flawed by the failure of humans in its execution. Represented by the Lady Justice statue whose blindfold, scale, and sword represent the equal administration of justice, it is up to each of us to hold leaders to its standards.

The combination of **political freedom** and the **free enterprise system** created and supports the most prosperous economy in world history. The Pilgrims initially implemented a socialist system at Plymouth, shedding it upon its failure and turning to the rewards of individual industry in capitalism. Individuals benefitting from opportunity instead of looking for entitlements incented deferred gratification and contributed to societal and personal advancement.

***

Though more diverse today, our founding based on the Judeo-Christian heritage of Western civilization, which advanced religion, art, architecture, technology, philosophy, and the early abolition of slavery, provided us a springboard from which to hasten our ascent among nations.

Our culture historically celebrates our faith and history milestones, including **Christmas, Easter, Chanukah or Hanukkah, Independence Day** (which some water down its importance by saying happy July 4th), and **Columbus Day,** among others. Unless you have been on another planet or under a rock, you're aware of the relentless assault on every traditional holiday our culture celebrates.

***

In summary:

- Our principles are unique from previous civilizations blended to maximize individual freedom and minimize government in citizens' lives.
- Unfortunately, humanity is flawed, illustrating the need to limit human power. There are too many illustrations of failed execution of our principles to enumerate here.
- The answer to restoring our principles and exceptional culture is a return to the complete adherence to the founding doctrines, elimination of career politicians, and less government, not more.

SECTION TWO

LEARNING AND LEADING

"Great leaders encourage leadership development by openly developing themselves."

—Marshall Goldsmith

PRINCIPLED VS. POWER LEADERSHIP

Today we're watching an epic struggle between principled leaders and those utilizing raw power to "bully" people into submission. People who decry bullying are often the same ones who stifle others' free speech if they find it disagreeable.

What happened to the time when everyone could speak their minds, and the marketplace of ideas would decide which one(s) were worthy of adopting? Spirited discussions where people voice their opinions and their information sources are healthy and develop stronger individuals on both sides of every issue. As we're told in Proverbs 27:17, "As iron sharpens iron, so one person sharpens another."

Conversely, if one side of an issue is the only one allowed and considered, individuals and our country suffer from the atrophy resulting from an inexperienced debate. Do we think business and political leaders in other countries will grant us any concessions in our dealing because we're not as experienced debating a wide range of ideas thoroughly? I don't think so, and their past and current behavior confirm my belief.

Former presidential candidate Adlai Stevenson stated, "The first principle in a free society is an untrammeled flow of words in an open forum." How long can we remain free without open debate and the free flow of ideas?

***

Americans adhering to principles developed over millennia by millions of people enabled us to produce the most prosperous nation in the history of the world. Our founders selected the most ethical components of Western civilization in other countries to establish our government.

The U.S. Constitution was written with checks and balances and limited power to prevent one or a small number of people from exercising too much power. The founders correctly realized rules only limit tyrants when the people and representatives are virtuous and enforce them. Orderly provisions for modification were enacted to make change deliberative, slow, and desired by many people instead of fast, significant, and decreed by any individual.

***

Principled leadership promotes honesty, one right and wrong, one truth, and principles over power. It recognizes human nature has not changed over time. Power is seductive. Lord Acton warned us, "Power corrupts, and absolute power corrupts absolutely." The founders didn't include term limits in the Constitution because no one at that time could afford to serve an extended amount of time. Instead of officeholders profiting from future lobbying, television, or think-tank opportunities, they returned home to continue their professions and lives.

Now, lawmakers often view elected office in Washington as a lifetime career. We only have to look at career politicians who leave office when they die because of their false perception of their irreplaceability. If one does retire, they rarely return home but capitalize on their contacts as stated above.

***

As politics has invaded every institution and the money involved has skyrocketed, people seeking and governing based on power politics have grown exponentially. They are often personally ambitious and play the game to win whatever it takes every day.

The "ends justify the means" triumphs over principles. Truth is the first casualty; as they say, whatever it takes at the moment is practiced, and they will change their position on any issue based on what is needed to win at any given moment.

Rules are another constraint that is thrown away on a whim if it brings an immediate victory. Power over principle sacrifices deliberating an issue and considering it example and precedent. Winning is all that matters in every situation.

The truth is to be defined by each individual as "his or her" truth. There is no absolute right and wrong, and morals are relative to the desire of today.

Do-gooder politicians view human nature as evolving and becoming better with each additional dollar they take from taxpayers and spends on those selected by the government to win.

Citizens are disrespected and treated as children who are only capable of surviving with government decision-making and taxpayer dollars. Dividing people into groups and creating jealousy weakens our country but serves power-hungry politicians who yearn for more control over individuals. Leader's practice "command and control" tactics and seldom trust others with power.

***

When moral leaders leave political, civic, or business office, they apply themselves to other efforts to contribute to their communities and prepare for future leadership. Servant leadership is a byproduct of moral life. People recognize how their predecessors contributed to their opportunities and look to "return the favor" to those who follow us. They make longer-range decisions based on their lifetime and beyond, the interests of others, and their creator. The future is more critical than any single moment.

President George Washington could have been king for life but voluntarily ceded power by advocating the position of president and retiring after two terms. As evidenced by Sam

Rayburn, President Ronald Reagan, and Joshua Chamberlain, principled leaders come from all political parties. Business and civic leaders include Sam Walton, Ernest Shackleton, and Billy Graham.

Power-hungry leaders rule rather than lead when in power and often undermine their superiors when they are not in control. They usually profit from their position, hold office until their last breath, and arrogantly feel entitled to special privileges because of their title.

General Benedict Arnold threw away a successful career and bright future in a power grab that's failure made his name synonymous with the word "traitor." Bernie Madoff abused his clients for personal gain. Current, longtime elected officials can be easily spotted by comparing their past and present positions on issues whether their party is in power or not. Too often, they reveal their preference of exercising power over morality most of the time.

***

America's promise of individual freedom to pursue life, liberty, and happiness was unique when launched and unmatched in the opportunities it affords us despite our human failings. The government was ordained to serve people, not rule over them.

We lived by The Golden Rule, "Do unto others as you would have them do unto you." We trusted people to be honest and righteous.

Citizens raised expectations and standards of individual performance in every generation, and people performed better to provide their children more prosperous lives. We celebrated personal achievement rather than promoting collectivist thinking.

Economist and philosopher Adam Smith recognized an "invisible hand" where individuals pursuing their interests unknowingly contributed to the greater good of society. Success did not rely on extensive government intrusion as politicians eager to wield power and control activity, and people would lead us to believe. He is discredited today by those thinking human nature has changed and invalidated his philosophy and celebrated by those understanding the consistency of human nature and the relevance of his theory throughout time.

***

If we want to continue our lives as free people, we must act instead of ignoring the growing chasm between principled people and those hungry for power.

***

What Can We Do to Empower More Principled Leaders and Fewer Power-Hungry Leaders?
1. Live principled lives.
2. Support, encourage, and vote for moral leaders at every opportunity.
3. Lead by example when we have the chance.
4. Live with the restraint of rules established using our governing documents.
5. Teach our children and those under our leadership principles and values over ambition and power.
6. We must inspire future generations to benefit from individual liberty gifted to them by generations who won and preserved it for us/them.
7. We must expose the deceit of all who use and abuse power for individual and political gain at the expense of individual liberty.

THE MOST UNDERREPORTED FACTOR THAT
SLOWED THE COVID-19 RECOVERY

Can one thing substantially influence our daily lives, slow progress, increase costs, and tilt the field of justice?

***

The phone rang. When I answered it, my excitement rose as I heard the banker greet me. He informed me the bank decided to accept my proposal. I completed the order form and submitted it to the factory. There were no signatures from either party on the agreement.

As I celebrated the largest order of my early career, the transaction's simplicity escaped me. Neither the banker nor I had any worries about the other party fulfilling their word and the arrangement.

Fast-forwarding to 2020, legal oversight, formal documentation, rigid processing rules, a formal fulfillment process, and concern about receiving timely payments delay business deals.

Yes, there were many benefits in those bygone days.

***

The most underreported factor that delayed the recovery from COVID-19 was businesses avoiding the risk of lawsuits based on current laws. Why couldn't we modify the decree to rebuild our economy and prevent the risk of systemic financial devastation?

We could, but politicians subordinated commonsense problem-solving to political calculations in an election year.

***

Why didn't the media report on this issue? Balanced stories informing the public of this issue and its impact would have inspired people to demand their elected officials act promptly and rebalance liability laws for all parties. More businesses would have re-opened and better served the public.

***

It wasn't too long ago when people consummated business and personal transactions with a handshake like the story above. On the rare occasion when things went awry, both parties solved any issue with honor.

I'm grateful to have experienced that time when it was rare to have any legal involvement in the business. We could verbally obtain commitments and fulfill them, with the only document being an invoice. Both sides operated with integrity and resolved the exceptional mistakes in a manner that increased respect and trust among all parties.

Times changed, and not for the better in this case. Now, lawyers for both sides counsel every contract to be bulletproof based on a perfectly legal environment. The results are delayed agreements, increased costs, less trust among parties, and more disagreements about every little technicality during the administration of the pact.

Business leaders factor the legal argument into the business case and determine a decision. In the COVID-19 environment, executives risked not just a failed arrangement but potentially a career-ending outcome. Very few can stand up to the legal and career pressure, which results in less progress and more inertia. Everyone surrounding a stalled deal suffers in addition to the principals. Customers miss life-improving products, suppliers suffer delayed or lost business, and people in the future lose or wait longer for new byproduct innovations.

The singular quest to WIN on every deal supersedes honor, trust, integrity, and the pursuit of a just transaction.

***

Common sense tells us life has risks, and none of us will get out of here alive. We cannot avoid all the risks of life regardless of who runs the government.

It is in the long-term interests of everyone to operate honestly and ethically. Failure to do so ruins their brand and the reputation of all who work in the field of commerce.

For markets to flourish, both sides must share equally the risks associated with their transactions.

***

I would submit the scale of risk for re-opening the economy during COVID-19 was tilted away from businesses and institutions and toward individuals. If we could have returned risks more evenly for lawsuits to a standard where gross negligence was required, we would have seen a dramatic increase in companies opening and growing their enterprise. Since politicians retained the lower threshold of a plaintiff proving negligence to win a suit, more businesses retreated into their shell of legal counsel until the pandemic ends.

Unfortunately for the country and each of us, there is a tipping point of no return for organizations that can't survive. We all lose when operations fail, whether it be immediately or in the long run. Conversely, we all win when commerce thrives directly or in the long run.

I don't know about you, but I'm for all sides winning now and in the future.

***

What Can We Do to Return Balance and Decency to Business?

1. Balance risks and rewards of transactions through modified liability laws.
2. Return **Common Sense** in our dealings with each other.
3. Return **Honor**, **Principle**, **Integrity**, and **Ethics** in our conduct.
4. Return **Individual Responsibility** to our character by educating everyone on the cost litigation adds to everything in our lives.
5. If we can restore 1-3, we can return legal concerns to a lesser part of life's events.

Our forefathers lived lives with honor, principle, integrity, personal ethics, responsibility, and common sense, so I know it can be done by us as well.

The question for us is whether we will rise to the occasion and reclaim those high ideals or further degrade into a dog-eat-dog world?

You Didn't Just Say That?

How often do you hear someone say something and shake your head in disbelief?

Depending on our life experiences, it happens at different frequencies and for distinctly contrasting communications.

***

I discovered many years ago some people purposely say provocative things to judge your reaction. When I began negotiating business deals with auto dealers, they demonstrated their proficiency in this area repeatedly. I joked with people if I had a nickel for every time a dealer insulted me before negotiations began, I would have wealth rivalling that of Jeff Bezos.

Not surprisingly, New Yorkers were the geographic champions with dealers in Chicago a close second as I described them as New York wannabes. They routinely questioned my heritage and honesty and my mother's reputation. Early on, I took each insult personally and was unable to conclude enough or profitable agreements successfully.

Finally, I realized the insults hurled at me in a seemingly unending stream were not personal but only a positioning tool to put me at a negotiating disadvantage. I finally concluded the buyers negotiated for sport, and the money in question came directly from their wallets. They are motivated by both financial and ego considerations. I altered my tactics resulting in more and better deals – and less stress. Their negotiations began at first contact and never ceased, even after prospects reached an initial agreement. I spent thirty years in the automotive industry and held the utmost respect for the business acumen of those in it.

***

When I observe politicians negotiating, it is a different atmosphere. Their primary motivation is one of ego:

1. They have no skin in the game as both sides barter with taxpayer money. Win or lose, they announce they won and proceed on to the next issue.
2. Few of them have ever negotiated anywhere but in a political environment. Politicians are used to trading quid quo pros with each other.
3. Losing face and political power are the only consequences they face from losing a bargain.

In the world of business, the stakes are much higher. Politicians are more willing to accept bad deals than no deal if it merely enhances their political standing.

When politicians face someone with real-world negotiating experience, they become exasperated like my early experiences. Finding their usual tactics ineffective, they flounder with emotional responses instead of calculated precision. It is common to hear them protest when they find themselves in an untenable position. Their realization they are not in control and are playing checkers in a chess game is hugely alarming.

***

Watching a master negotiator is a beautiful sight, especially if you're not on the other side of the table. They think multiple steps ahead in the transaction and routinely outmaneuver their opponents in doing so. Every communication impacts the recipient's eyes, ears, brain, and emotions. They communicate to multiple parties simultaneously in a way each party believes they are the only intended beneficiary. They handle speed changes in the negotiation like a pro fisherman lands a trophy fish. They position themselves for the current deal and future ones concurrently. Canceling at the last minute, no-showing, or storming out of a meeting are legitimate tactics to position ongoing communications. They obtain their objectives while allowing the other side to believe they won the deal. Observers often mistake their communications of strength as a weakness because of the viewers' lack of expertise.

***

An example of these skills occurred in 2019 when President Trump negotiated a trade deal with China. An added feature to this accord was he transacted so many of the communications in public.

As negotiations continued, the media responded to each exchange as if it indicated how the deal would conclude. As so often is the case, it is normal not to know the actual result until the paper's ink dries. Twists, turns, ups, downs, starts, and stops are routine.

During the discussions, President Trump said that the United States would not meet with China because "China is not ready to meet with us yet." On the surface, the statement appeared to place the U.S. in weakness like China did not want to meet until the U.S. conceded to them. In reality, based on classic Trump negotiating strategies, he was signaling to the Chinese that the U.S. would not meet with them until they moved their posture toward the American position. The media trumpeted how China had manipulated the president into a weak position. In reality, the U.S. position was strong, borne out when President Trump concluded the deal in favor of the American people.

***

Although we don't negotiate personally in commerce as much we used to do, it is a normal part of everyday life. We still deal when buying our homes and cars, as they are usually our largest purchases. But, when was the last time you negotiated the purchase of clothes, insurance, or other services.

We negotiate jobs and raises and in our interpersonal relationships. While we rarely shock someone to open negotiations, posturing begins early and is ongoing during the relationship. When my daughter, Elizabeth, was only six months old, I detected her negotiating for food and drink by her responses to what we presented her. From that point forward, her skills continue to grow.

Do you accept a middle seat assignment on an airplane without haggling for a more desirable location? How many times do you request special treatment by asking someone, "can you throw in some extra X?" Who hasn't asked for an upgraded hotel room, airplane seat, class of cabin on a cruise ship, or any number of other products and services? Did you and your siblings haggle over taking out the trash, washing the dishes, or doing other household chores?

We all have room to enhance our skills to negotiate better, more often, and make the experience more profitable and pleasant.

***

How Can We Better Negotiate in Life?
1. Know the arena you are negotiating your transaction. Is it a personal relationship? Business?
2. Know the customs in each arena's transactions.
3. Know as much as possible about the person(s) in the transaction/relationship.
4. Know your objective, acceptable contingencies, and walk away points.
5. Plan several steps in your strategy based on alternative responses in the discussion.
6. Reach all parties with your communications.
7. Be calm under pressure and through the uncertainties of the process.

8. Debate one transaction with a long-term perspective of multiple agreements.
9. No deal is always better than a bad deal.

Ironically, the best negotiators in their personal lives are most averse to negotiating in business. Conversely, some who are proficient in business deals are less capable in intimate relationships. The bottom line is negotiating skills are painfully learned and require a lifetime commitment to develop fully.

THE 5 LEADERSHIP SECRETS OF
OLD MACDONALD

What can we learn from Old MacDonald beyond the song, even if we're not a farmer? The song is believed to date back to the 1720s English folk music. Most of us sang it as children.

Old MacDonald had a farm, E-I-E-I-O,
And on his farm, he had a cow, E-I-E-I-O,
With a moo-moo here and a moo-moo there,
Here a moo,
there a moo,
everywhere moo-moo,
Old MacDonald had a farm, E-I-E-I-O.

We missed the most important leadership lessons we can learn from Old MacDonald. It wasn't the cow, pig, duck, and horse that made him successful. I think I broke the code and discovered the secret of his success!

All the time, It was the E-I-E-I-O!

Did you ever wonder what e-i-e-i-o in the song meant? If you're like me, I believed I was too big a boy to sing it by the time I cared.

However, Old MacDonald's secret to being a successful farmer lies in those melodious letters. If we look more closely, we can discover their meaning and use them to help our journey in life.

The first E is, for **Example**. MacDonald knew the best leadership was by example. He also knew everyone is an example to others regardless of their age, station-in-life, or willingness. He lived Albert Schweitzer's wise words, which said, "Example is not the main thing in influencing others, it's the only thing." MacDonald's was an example in three ways for all to see:

1. He was **honest** in all of his business dealings. His word was his bond.
2. He **worked hard** in everything he did. MacDonald arrived at work first and left last inspiring others to exert additional effort.
3. MacDonald was a **team player**. He realized the sum of each team member's effort exceeded its raw total due to a phenomenon called "synergy." In other words, $2+2 = 5$ in an equation where the team works together.

The first I is for **Instruction.** MacDonald knew his team required instruction to achieve maximum results. As the leader, he was responsible for planning and administrating transformative lessons for his team. He believed Maria Montessori's advice, "the best instruction is that which uses the fewest words sufficient for the task.

MacDonald used three principles to instruct his team:

1. The foundation of successful leadership is **Vision.** Without it, no teaching or plan will succeed.
2. MacDonald realized **Good communications** were essential to convey the best of visions and plans.
3. Without **Solid "how-to" techniques** to implement plans, good communications are unsuccessful.

The second E is for **Encourager.** MacDonald knew his team didn't care how much he knew until he showed them how much he cared for them. He utilized the philosophy that "A word of encouragement during a failure is worth more than an hour of praise after a success" – as found in Encouragement quotes.

MacDonald employed three characteristics to maximize the effectiveness of his encouragement on his team's performance.

He **listened** when team members voiced their concerns, opinions, and needs. An effective leader can separate constructive from detrimental feedback to adapt an organization for increased success.

MacDonald **complimented efforts and achievements** in public in the appreciation of the team's extraordinary exertion.

He lifted team members when confronted with adversity to **persevere through the pain** until they achieved their objective.

The second I is for **Inspiration.** MacDonald utilized a coaching leadership style for lifting his team's performance beyond what they believed they could achieve. Anyone can lead in easy times, but the best leaders inspire their teams to succeed through good and bad times. Walt Disney overcame much adversity and inspired us, stating, "**All our dreams can come true if we have the courage to pursue them.**"

MacDonald communicated three types of stories to inspire his team:

1. He told **stories of the successes of others** to show his team members could achieve their objectives.
2. MacDonald told **stories of others overcoming adversity** to lift and reignite his team when misfortune knocked them down.
3. He told **stories of seizing opportunity** after his team members achieved success to spur them to heights they never believed they could achieve.

Finally, the only O stands out for MacDonald's **Optimism.** Farming is a feast or famine lifestyle necessitating an optimistic attitude to persevere through drought, flood, storms, pestilence, predators, and numerous other daily threats. Helen Keller, who knew something about experiencing adversity and challenges, shared words that enabled her to achieve much more than anyone believed possible. She said, "Optimism is the faith that leads to achievement. Nothing can be done without hope and confidence."

MacDonald's optimism was the capstone of his successful leadership disciplines. He lived three characteristics common to successful people:

1. Like Keller, MacDonald maintained a **positive attitude** through good times and bad, which empowered him to move forward continually.

2. He had a **sense of humor** that enabled him to laugh when others might cry at misfortune. It prepared him to get back up every time he was knocked down and resume his quest for success. Could you have E-I-E-I-O so prominently in the song without a sense of humor?

3. MacDonald **enjoyed life daily**. My observation and experience are the happiest and most successful people enjoy every day regardless of the circumstances they experience. They always find the good in everything. They experience joy and radiate it to others they encounter.

Remember, the cow, duck, pig, and horse didn't make Old MacDonald successful without the E-I-E-I-O!

Whether we are farmers or not, if we practice E-I-E-I-O like Old MacDonald daily, we will achieve a happier, more successful, and more fulfilling life's journey.

Rules, We Don't Need No Stinking Rules

What? The heck, you say!

This title is a play on the *Blazing Saddles'* scene when the bandits say, "Badges? We don't need no stinking badges" while being recruited for a posse.

The U.S. Constitution is the oldest governing document in operation in the entire world. It has functioned well, limiting excessive political reach since written in 1787 and ratified in 1788.

***

Our form of government has never been under more direct attack than it is today. The brilliance of separation of powers, checks and balances, respect of debate to include minority opinions, and limited government authority to specific enumerated powers was borne from men, though imperfect, who distrusted human nature from experience and study.

John Adams rightly said, "If men were angels, no government would be necessary." His attitude was the gold standard amongst the founders.

George Washington was so popular he could have been king or president for as long as he wished. He knew the temptation of unbridled power. His precedent of serving only two terms stood until 1940. Franklin Roosevelt disregarded the example and added a fourth term in 1944.

***

Today, politicians at all levels of government have forgotten Washington and his example. They swell with power, hold office for entire careers, and often only leave feet first.

Are any of them, or us, indispensable to any organization? Absolutely not!

We have to be careful how much government we desire because we will get it and more!

As government grows at unabated warp speed, our individual liberties vanish as quickly.

***

Early in our history, voters held elected officials closely accountable with shorter terms of office. Joshua Chamberlain, for example, was elected governor of Maine four times and served a total of four years! The duration of office was one year!

Since then, elected officials have fooled the electorate, saying the cost of running for office and time campaigning are so onerous they deserved longer terms. Voters bought the pitch, which also contributes to officeholders remaining so long their perspectives migrate from being public servants to the masses' rulers.

That difference in attitude is ever-increasingly manifesting itself into insensitive politicians whose actions reveal influence by special interest groups represented by well-funded lobbyists and career staff personnel.

The fourth estate of the media has transformed from the watchdog of American liberty to active partisan participants in public policy, which conceals the ruling class ever gaining power.

***

See if you recognize the symptoms of my argument.

During the 2020 COVID-19 pandemic, politicians grabbed power swiftly and aggressively because the health issue was an "emergency." The problem is human nature drives elected officials to grab power more quickly than to relinquish it.

Within days of his inauguration, President Biden bypassed Congress and signed 56 executive orders. This continued a trend from past-presidents of increasing the power of the executive branch at the expense of the legislative and judicial branches of government.

Our system does not authorize anyone person to exercise that amount of power. Unfortunately, few in Congress, states, or courts have shown the strength to stop the lawless power grab. The precedent is dangerous for our future!

Only 9 percent of the breathtaking nearly $2 trillion 2021 relief bill for the pandemic went to COVID-related issues. The remainder of the money went overseas or to political allies. Leadership stifled the debate. They also discarded bi-partisanship approval for power. "Never let a crisis go to waste" is a political maxim that should scare all of us.

When the Senate parliamentarian ruled modifying the minimum wage was not allowed by the rules with the process planned to approve the bill, the Speaker of the House and many representatives in Congress blasted to not listen to the ruling or get rid of the parliamentarian. In other words, damn the rules and full speed ahead. We want what we want, and we want it now! It sounds like a preschooler, doesn't it?

***

When I was a kid, my older cousin and I played Monopoly. Our younger brothers begged to play with us. Once we allowed them in the game, we changed the rules on every roll of the dice. We won all of the time!

Eventually, they realized the abuse and demanded their rights. When we played by set rules, the game was more fun for our brothers than for us.

Laws are guardrails against extreme swings in either direction and protect minority interests. They reduce the risk of wild swings in either direction, like bumpers in bowling.

***

Why would elected officials so openly flout rules in their quest to access more taxpayer money to distribute to their friends?

The only reason is they believe they are bulletproof and disrespect voters. Until they are concerned—dare I say, until they fear voters—they will proceed with impunity.

As the character Alan Moore said in *V for Vendetta*, "People shouldn't be afraid of their government. Governments should be afraid of their people."

***

Are you not convinced yet? Do you still believe officials spend a lifetime in "public service"? How many of them become multi-millionaires on "public servant" salaries? How in the name of mathematics does that happen?

While they say they are taking care of us, they almost always are really taking care of themselves and their families. C. S. Lewis said, **"Of all the tyrannies, a tyranny sincerely exercised for the good of its victims may be the most oppressive."**

***

Now, I sense your attention! What can we do?

No one of us can do everything, but we all can do one thing. Nobel laureate and Holocaust survivor Elie Wiesel said, "One person of integrity can make a difference." Wiesel certainly maximized his contributions to the world after surviving the Holocaust.

We can and should find our passion and act! Each of us who invests our citizenship efforts will honor our forefathers and gift our descendants with the precious gift of political and economic freedom we have received.

Thomas Jefferson gave us the best prescription for life, saying, "I predict future happiness for Americans if they can prevent the government from wasting the labors of the people under the pretense of taking care of them."

***

What efforts can we promote and participate in to "make a difference?"

1. Lobby your state elected officials to call **The Convention of States** as prescribed in Article 5 of The U. S. Constitution.
    *   It will enable non-elected officials to advocate congressional term limits.
    *   It will help states re-establish their authority.
2. Advocate **Term Limits** at every level of elected politics.
    *   Rotating elected officials brings new ideas and reduces entrenched officeholders.
3. Advocate **Ethics reform.** Prevent elected officials from becoming lobbyists.
    *   Prevent elected officials from officially interacting with relatives in the media, lobbyists, and agencies.
4. Advocate the Re-establishment of **election integrity** with these and other rules.
    *   Without specific rules to prevent fraud, elections don't matter.
    *   Voter ID
    *   Limit mail-in and absentee balloting.
    *   Paper ballots for audit trails.
    *   Machine ballots with paper backup, not connected to the internet.
5. Re-establish the balance in the **separation of powers** between branches of the federal government.
6. Re-establish **Federalism** between the U.S. government and the states.

We, the people, get the government we demand. As citizens, our rights will only remain as long as we exercise our responsibilities.

Playing the Hand You're Dealt

Encouragement for Enduring Change and Adversity

The phrase "death and taxes are the only two certain things in life" dates to the early 1700s. My suggestion is to add **change** and **adversity** to the list. Change in nearly everything is inevitable and impacts us throughout life. Everyone is challenged by adversity in varying degrees and severity in their lifetime.

***

Charles F. Stanley tells us, "You can't always avoid adversity. But you can always choose how you respond to it." His wise words apply to change and adversity equally because they often appear as the same thing. If we don't learn to respond to change and adversity, our lives will be miserable each time we encounter them.

***

When we were preparing for my daughter Elizabeth's birth, we discovered the book, *On Becoming Babywise*, which promoted training babies to sleep through the night within two months of birth. As most parents would agree, that marketing line was enticing.

The secret was not to automatically comfort the baby immediately after he or she cried for attention. Doing so would affirm the behavior by teaching the baby that the world revolved around him or her. Instead, the baby needed to learn how to fit into the world.

Elizabeth's mother wisely added the discipline, "if you cry for something, you don't get it," to her upbringing. She has matured into a well-adjusted young lady. I attribute a significant contributor to her character to these two parenting techniques.

When I see young adults throw temper tantrums, require safe spaces, and protest someone triggering them, I see individuals I envision were spoiled with too much attention and treated with too much importance when they were young. They believe the world should adjust to their desires instead of adjusting how they fit into and contribute to society. They are often miserable because there is no way the real world will ever meet their expectations.

***

A noteworthy example whose adaptation and walk of life is worthy of emulation is Joni Erickson Tada. Her life choices changed in an instant as an eighteen-year-old.

A diving accident left Joni paralyzed from the neck down. There was no time to prepare for a different future or receive a do-over. Joni faced a monumental change, and adversity rolled into the same event and its lifetime impact.

Her choice was to wallow in self-pity or discover a new and more significant purpose for her life. Joni's faith is instrumental in her view of life. She receives encouragement during down days from Romans 5:3-5 – "Not only so, but we also glory in our sufferings, because we know that suffering produces perseverance; perseverance, character; and character, hope. And hope does not put us to shame because God's love has been poured out into our hearts through the Holy Spirit, who has been given to us." Over time, like countless others, she finds purpose, comfort, and provision in *The Holy Bible*.

***

Joni has dedicated her life to Christian ministry. While she emphasizes the disabled community, her example and efforts positively impact all fortunate enough to receive them. She has authored more than forty-eight books, hosts the *Joni and Friends* radio program, performs music, and is an artist.

She is relentless and fearless in her activities. She states, "Deny your weakness, and you will never realize God's strength in you." She recognizes, "All you really need is the One who promised never to leave or forsake you – the One who said, 'I am with you always.' Evidence of the validity of those two statements is the staggering volume and impact of her work.

She continues to create and contribute to the world. Her refusal to allow her disability to disable her illustrates Clemson football coach Dabo Swinney's statement, "The only disability is a bad attitude."

Too often, public attention focuses on those who complain and invest their time destroying what others have built. To succeed in the future, we need people who desire to build upon their predecessors' contributions.

***

Joni overcoming her accident and channeling her energy into positive efforts shows us all obstacles don't have to defeat us. She is tenaciously pursuing her objectives despite challenges most of us don't experience. Lost to time is the eloquent author who brilliantly recognized, "It is amazing what you can do when you don't know what you can't do."

***

Another characteristic of Joni is her priority on serving the needs of others. Her heart is one of a servant-leader. I know the value of this from personal experience when I have encountered suffering. When I concentrate on my situation, it is easy for me to feel depressed. But, when I turn my attention to using my incident to help others, I feel better and positively contribute to society.

When we turn our difficulties into service for others, we lift them from wherever they are, raise their hope for the future, and influence their faith in their fellow man.

***

How Do We Endure and Thrive Through Any Change or Adversity?

1. Recognize we must fit into the world as it is. The world will not adjust to our demands.
2. Demanding safe spaces and non-triggering words or crying will not inspire people to surrender to your demands in real life.
3. Realize a setback or failure is not an end to your dreams but is an opportunity to deepen and broaden your experience and refine your objectives. Often, one reversal redirects us to become more successful than we would have without the misfortune.
4. People with a positive attitude are contagious. They draw others toward those who exhibit it. No one wants to hang out with negative people.
5. Relentlessly pursue your dreams despite any real or perceived obstacles. More often than not, you will overcome difficulties and succeed.
6. When we focus our energy on serving others, we lose sight of our problems and positively impact individuals and the future.
7. When we properly adjust to changes and adversity, we provide the best example to those coming behind us.

***

Life is challenging enough without our approaching it with the misconception it owes us anything and will deter its course for our demands. Without the proper understanding of this fact and learning to assimilate with society, we will never achieve happiness.

When Tested, "Hang Tough"!

When adversity appears, how do we respond?

***

None of us like facing tough times. We would rather our lives progress in comfort and ease, gradually becoming more and more happy and prosperous. Unfortunately, only in fictional literature is that elusive possibility an option.

Life blessed some of us to experience minimal hardships as we grew up, and others hit the ground in a fight for their lives. If we're fortunate, difficulties come and go during life, and if we're unfortunate, it finds us daily. Some challenges appear in an instant, and we can deal with them just as quickly. Some miseries seem to last an eternity and resist every response to dispatch them forever into our memories.

There are two crucial questions regarding our response to the troubles we encounter. First, how do we respond? Second, do we learn anything from each affliction that helps us successfully engage and eliminate it?

Do we run and hide, hoping the issue will go away and we can avoid it? Do we stand and face it only to respond insufficiently to overcome its force? Or, are we able to withstand the attack and victoriously repel it with calm and confidence?

If we're candid, we have probably responded in each way one time or another. We can hope, as we age and accumulate more life experiences, we will better address each tribulation.

***

I have failed more than once in my response to adversity. I hope my answers have improved through experience. I'll relate one failure I was fortunate to survive through no merit of mine.

On June 10, 1977, I was awakened just after 5 in the morning by a banging on my apartment door. Dazed, I answered the door to see an out-of-breath fireman who screamed for me to get out of the building.

As I retreated into my apartment, he continued to yell for me to drop everything and "get out!" Since I saw no fire and very little smoke, I went to the bathroom, put my contacts into my eyes, and grabbed one box containing my coin collection.

The fireman became apoplectic! "Get out NOW!"

I exited my apartment. Instead of turning left to the quickest exit, I turned right toward the parking lot, which was my routine. The fireman screamed again and then smartly exited the closest door I had ignored.

As I later learned, I was the last person out of the sixteen-unit building. My neighbor, who fell asleep and started the fire with his cigarette, died. As the crow flies, authorities found his body less than thirty feet from my bedroom. The fireman told me how fortunate I was to escape the smoke. He informed me the gas from burning plastic can kill someone within thirty seconds. In addition to tasting smoke with every breath for several days, I was thankful to survive.

I lived to face the next test because the Lord protected me, not because of my brilliant response to the fire.

***

My dad was part of the greatest generation who grew up during the depression and came of age during World War II. I always thought he was tough enough to overcome any disaster.

He lived a can-do spirit and taught it to me relentlessly as often and in as many different methods as he could. When I said I couldn't do something, he instinctively replied, "can't never did anything." I didn't understand the basis of his lesson as early as I wish I would have.

After his passing in 2007, I learned some of the boyhood experiences he hadn't shared with me.

When he was about ten or eleven, my grandfather dropped Dad off to work in a field on a remote farm while my grandfather worked land quite a distance away. Unforeseen circumstances kept my grandfather from retrieving Dad at the end of the day.

Without preparation or provision, events compelled Dad to spend the night in a wagon at the edge of the field. Not only did he lack food and water, but he also had no access to a radio, cell phone, book, or anything else to keep him company. I wish I would have known this story and been able to discuss his thoughts during that extra-long night.

The next day, my grandfather rescued him. I'm sure he was overjoyed seeing his dad. This experience was only one of the untold number of occasions he lived that contributed to his self-reliant, can-do spirit.

***

I learned of the exceptional service of Easy Company, 506th Parachute Regiment, of the 101st Airborne Division during World War II through the ***Band of Brothers*** book and later mini-series. They were a minuscule fraction of men and women who served during the war, but the show spotlighted their service.

Major Richard "Dick" Winters began the war as a lieutenant but rose in rank because of his exceptional leadership skills. One soldier after another gave him credit for their success and survival during post-war interviews.

His motto of "Hang tough" resounded in his troops at the arrival of every obstacle, enemy engagement, and loss. Beginning in Normandy on D-day June 6, 1944, through the end of the war when they arrived at Berchtesgaden, Germany, at Adolph Hitler's Eagles Nest, Winters' leadership and example were on display.

Major Winters' leadership was honored on June 6, 2012, with the dedication of the Major Richard "Dick" Winters "Hang

Tough" statue at Sainte-Marie-du-Mont, honoring all of the junior officers who led combat troops on D-Day.

Winters succeeded as a leader because he led from the front. He cared for his troops, and, in addition to accomplishing their missions, he exhibited a strong example for others in any endeavor.

***

In the days discussed above, the risk was an expected and accepted part of life. When challenges appeared, you sucked it up, faced it head-on, and learned from the experience, whether successful or not.

There was no entitlement of a do-over, bailout, or government rescue. Sometimes you won, other times you lost, and the rest you were glad to live to tell others about it.

***

How can we face challenges, overcome them, and better prepare for unknown future tests?
1. Learn and remember the lessons from past trials. Prepare for the unexpected. Don't panic when misfortune arrives.
2. Withstanding the first blow of the catastrophe is essential in answering it successfully.
3. While you're suffering trouble's attack, recall your past successful responses to hardships.
4. Identify people you can ask for help.
5. Others will always observe your actions in a crisis. Your efforts will influence their opinion of you.
6. After overcoming hard times, give thanks. Appreciate your increase in confidence to meet the next affliction you face.

***

I believe most of us have parents, grandparents, and forefathers who experienced challenging events. Those episodes collectively contributed to their Ameri-"can" do spirit. They built the most prosperous country in the history of the world. We stand on their broad shoulders today. To retain the freedom we have enjoyed, we must recapture the American spirit, discard reliance on the government for our welfare, and stop blaming others for our misfortunes.

WHO DECIDES THE MOST IMPORTANT DECISION OF THE YEAR?

The Most Important Decisions are Always the Toughest Ones to Make

As we navigated the COVID-19 pandemic, most of us encountered choices never faced before. Additionally, those decisions may be the most important life decisions we ever make.

The peace, tranquility, and comfort of 2020 quickly gave way to anxiety, fear, worry, and doubt with the arrival in March of the Coronavirus. Not since the 1917-1920 Spanish flu pandemic covered the globe has anyone confronted similar challenges.

Yes, the Spanish flu arrived during World War I. Our parents and grandparents also endured it and survived the Great Depression, World War II, and the Cold War during their lives. As great as all of those afflictions were, they each differed from the global health threat they faced.

We usually suffer individually or in small groups.

1. All of experienced this pandemic simultaneously. The diversity of our responses to the same event is highly instructive. It will continue to impact our futures beyond the time when this virus is but a memory.

Contemplating students and teachers returning to school for in-person instruction was a complicated decision. In a typical cost-benefit analysis, we can compare the health risks of in-person instruction to the reduced benefit of virtual classwork and make an educated, logical decision. In a laboratory, we can complete the exercise in minutes.

In reality, three gigantic parameters affected the back-to-school question with a disproportionate influence on the outcome. They illustrate a universal principle that our **most important decisions are always the toughest ones to make**.

First, **human emotions will impact each facet of every decision**. Parents, children, teachers, administrators, and government leaders all have biases based on who the decision affects and the perceived risks associated with their agendas.

Second, the **Government is ineffective at every level** because one size does not fit all. That is the only solution method known to the public sector. Politicians infuse every decision with political calculations instead of merely basing decisions on health concerns.

Third, **it was imperative parents and school boards closest to students decided when to return to in-person instruction**. As with any other public decision, the ones made closer to the people who can personally interact and hold accountable the decision-makers are the best. Unless we're large donors, it is virtually impossible to have a substantial discussion with members of the U.S. Congress, anyone in Washington, D.C., or at the state level.

People closest to each student and teacher can individualize decisions providing exceptions to broad-brushed bureaucratic edicts. Schools were re-opened safely for the majority and gave the best experience for this school year and each student's future. Exceptions for students and teachers with high-risk factors were permitted them to have the best possible virtual experience until the decline of their risk enabled them to return to the classroom.

Limited powers for any individual and any governmental body and solid checks-and-balances to protect the people is our country's foundation. We must resist the attraction of speed and simplicity from one autocrat at any level issuing a blanket decree.

Why Would We Give Up Citizenship for Subjection in the name of Equity?

You're probably too aware of the constant political squabbling on every issue in our country. It's annoying, aggravating, and intrusive in our daily lives. You may or may not recognize it is only a symptom of a mortal threat to our individual liberty that has been in process actively since the Vietnam protest days.

***

I first noticed the poisonous attack on our country and Western civilization as a freshman at The University of Texas at Austin in the spring of 1970. Curious, I went to the plaza in front of the iconic Tower on campus to observe a protest against the Vietnam War. Mixed in with the chants to bring the troops home was another rhythmic message saying, "Hey hey, ho ho, Western civ has got to go." I was puzzled at the mixed messaging but later realized it was a standard component of all left-wing protest activities. Everyone with a grievance was allowed to voice their anger to increase the numbers and volume emanating from the mob.

***

Since those days, there have been steady streams of left-wing protests on various issues. One component of many of them is the movement to water down the difference between citizenship, and residents, aliens, and occupants. There is a substantial and unique difference for us in the United States that bad actors are purposefully obscuring to transform our country from its founding principles into another form more detrimental to our liberty.

***

Because too many of our citizens take their rights for granted, we need to review our unique status to ensure we pass our gift along to future generations. We fail to do so at our peril.

1. Anyone can be a subject to a government, whether it is a monarchy, left or right-wing dictatorship, or another other autocratic configuration. We merely need to obey all the orders we're given and don't object to the fearless leader.
2. Very few people today, or in the history of man, have been blessed to be free citizens with individual political and economic freedom!
3. Our forefathers paid a hefty price initially and repeatedly to pass our gift of liberty to us!

Why you ask, is the difference significant and worth fighting and dying to preserve? Subjects are ruled by government, which is to say people who determine what rights to issue, what rights to withdraw, whom to bestow those rights upon, and extremely important, whom to withhold rights from as a punishment for non-compliance. People have minimal freedom and are frequently abused by power-hungry bureaucrats who receive pleasure exercising power more significantly than their wisdom deserves.

There is NO individual liberty without political and economic freedom.

***

Another phenomenon recent in history is the awarding of "dual citizenship," which further confuses people on the actual value of citizenship and allegiance to any one country. I believe it is another strategy used by some to promote eventual global government where everyone is subject to that authority.

For example, if one were a U.S. citizen and a subject of the United Kingdom, where would his or her loyalty predominantly rest? Each person would select their choice, but no one would be 100% loyal to either country.

***

Beyond anyone in history, American citizens live blessed lives in freedom. Everyone enjoys and desires their rights. Genuine rights are given by God eternally, and man cannot withdraw them. Some people demand government extend additional rights, but anything people as government agents provide can just as quickly be revoked. Why should we as a free people give away our God-given rights to the government (people) and let them believe they have the power to give and take away rights?

God-given rights make citizens free and masters of government rather than its servant.

***

As our republic has aged, many see rights as a perpetual entitlement. Easily forgotten is its price extracted from every generation to perpetuate it.

Many overlook the responsibilities of citizenship in the glow of its rights. To enjoy individual liberty and succeed as a country, we must:

1. To enjoy our freedom, we must accept the free action of those with whom we disagree.
2. We must defend our mutual freedom together as part of a social compact codified in our Constitution.
3. We must exercise our freedom by voting for our representatives, where each legal citizen has one vote.

4. Through our free individual efforts pursuing our dreams, we act with Adam Smith's "invisible hand" to build a better country for the future. We freely choose what, how much, when, where, and how we live, not a government bureaucrat.

***

Our founders were brilliant as they made individual citizens supreme in our country. People are citizens of states, and states representing us delegate power to the federal government with dominion over it. Unfortunately, we have allowed the national government to seize dominant power and, in doing so, restrict citizen and state liberty.

Those who crafted our founding structure and documents astutely understood human nature, which led to their dividing power into three branches and limiting the power of any one department, group, or individual.

The 2020 COVID-19 pandemic revealed how quickly individual politicians could and would seize and expand their power given any opportunity.

As Lord Acton said, "Power tends to corrupt, and absolute power corrupts absolutely." We must vigilantly restrict the power of individuals, groups, and government agencies, or we will find ourselves subjects rather than citizens.

***

Our individual liberty is under the most serious assault since the Revolutionary War. The push for equity is a direct attack on our freedom because a given to free people is we will each be different through our birth, talent, and efforts. Equity promises to make everyone equally the same, but no government can deliver upon that promise regardless of who leads it.

Though it has failed every time others attempted it, each subsequent demagogue believes and promises they can finally produce equity for all.

***

Another attack on our individual liberty is through the emotional appeal of collectivism. Leaders mix their theft of individual rights within legitimate community efforts. Anyone who asserts individualism receives savage attacks for an absence of empathy at best and selfishness as routine.

Our history is full of successful examples where people pursued their individual dreams and achieved momentous corporate achievements through their voluntary accumulation. Yes, consequential events such as World War II required a more collective approach, but we're more successful when it is the exception rather than the rule.

We must beware the actions and words of those who run for office to "help us." All help is not the same.

No leader devoted to collectivism will respect an individual's freedom of speech and religion, private property, and the right to self-defense.

Only leaders committed to individual liberty will honor those rights for citizens.

Only people with a history of respecting individual liberty are worthy of our support for public leadership positions.

***

Former Texas Secretary of State and Attorney General John Ben Shepperd, who was a friend and mentor of mine, said, "To be born free is an accident. To live free is a responsibility. To die free is an obligation.

***

We owe our freedom to those who sacrificed and built our great country. If we are to fulfill our obligation, we must:

1. Wake up to the active threat against our freedom.
2. Stand up and commit to act in at least one more area to defend our liberty.
3. Saddle up and ride to the sound of the threat.
4. Show up at the point of the threats to prevent them from succeeding.
5. Speak up because our action will embolden like-minded people to join us and strengthen our numbers when we speak.
6. Toughen up because our adversary plays long ball, and we will not defeat them in one action. We must persevere!
7. Stay up however long it takes to achieve total victory! Stay up with whatever it takes to restore our complete individual freedom! Stay up with whoever it takes to contribute to absolute victory!

Why would anyone give up our gift of individual liberty to be pulled down to an equality of mediocrity?

Why would we give away our right as a master of our government for a role of a subject?

Why would we sacrifice the gift purchased at such a high price for slavery to an all-powerful government led from either side of the political spectrum?

Every day we have the opportunity to contribute to the preservation of our liberty or let our inaction increase the threat to our freedom. The choice is ours every day.

I know what my choice is. What is yours?

THE MOST IMPORTANT CHARACTERISTIC
OF SUCCESSFUL LEADERS

There are thousands of books written over centuries about outstanding leadership. Speakers and trainers are paid handsomely by organizations to share principles of effective leadership. Successful leadership characteristics are well-proven and documented for anyone who wants to study them.

Yet, many who read the books and receive ample training do not demonstrate triumphant leadership skills.

I believe many reasons interfere with championship leadership, but I want to focus on one I have seen firsthand in multiple organizations.

Leaders who put themselves in front of their organization and people inject cancerous negativism into everything they touch. On the other hand, servant leaders instill positivism into everything they influence, even if they aren't masters of their craft.

It amazes me selfish leaders are usually oblivious to how obvious their self-centered actions are to everyone. President Theodore Roosevelt wisely observed, "People don't care how much you know until they know how much you care." Once perceived as selfish, a leader will find it nearly impossible to successfully lead a team to maximum performance.

On the other hand, when people know how much you care about them, and you are focused on achieving your mission and building them and your organization for future success, they will, figuratively speaking, run through a wall to contribute to the team's success. President Ronald Reagan proclaimed, "It is amazing what you can accomplish when you don't care who gets the credit." His team was highly loyal to him and worked diligently to achieve his vision during his presidency.

In politics, it is easy to spot selfish leaders by their actions and enrichment over time. President Harry S. Truman said, "An honest public servant can't become rich in politics. He can only attain greatness and satisfaction by service." There are too few honest politicians these days, but I naively hope to return to principled servant leadership.

In business, leadership actions can be less apparent, but selfish and servant leaders sometimes exist side-by-side. Unless the organization weeds out narcissistic leaders, it will never achieve its potential. Servant leaders achieve success also because they realize Zig Ziglar's wise words, "You can get anything you want out of life if you help enough other people get what they want." That attitude contributes to the leadership of organizations and people to succeed. It also elevates their esteem by others and achievement in the process.

Several studies find that more people quit their managers than other reasons for leaving a company.

Beth Williams of Prime East Forward Focus writes in the article "Poor *Leadership is the Number One Reason Your Employees Quit*" that the best managers understand their employees and drive personal development (i.e., growth). To do this, a manager needs a servant attitude rather than a self-centered heart and leadership style. The article describes the hundreds of billions of dollars businesses lose to employee turnover each year, confirming the advantage of having leaders with a serving approach.

What causes this drastic difference in the two types of leaders? I believe our self-centered human nature overwhelms the spirit of service in all of us sometimes and in some of us all of the time.

Those with servant attitudes and self-discipline cast aside their selfish instincts while others succumb to their narcissistic characteristics most of the time.

How do we differentiate the attributes between selfish and servant leaders? Below is a comparison. You'll recognize many, if not all of them, and visualize people you know who display traits in their daily activities.

Self-Centered vs. Servant Leader Traits

Self-Centered	Servant
What's in it for me and mine	How can I benefit others while leading them
Today is all that matters	Long-term view
Short-sighted considerations	Visionary for future impact
Decisions made independently, inconsistent	Decisions consider precedent
Wields power	Exercises power
Narcissist	Humble
Takes credit	Gives credit
Avoids responsibility	Takes responsibility
Ambitious for self	No self-ambition – Steps up when called
Loyal only to self	Loyal to others, and them to him/her
Seeks statues and their name on buildings	Seeks results not accolades
People are instruments to use for power	Grows people for future service
Entitled	Grateful
Poor example	Excellent example
Keeps score with money & their name on things	Leaves score to people lifted by relationship
Creates own truth	Lives the truth
Relative morality	Principled
Drains energy from subordinates	Positively energize subordinates
Held in contempt by others	Held in high esteem by others
Deserve different treatment because they are more important	Everyone is equal and valued team contributors

| Too big to do a small job | Will do any job to help the team |
| Micromanages stifling individuals | Empowers people to act |

Everyone I know would much rather work for and with a servant leader than a self-centered one.

Will this piece make any difference in our future actions? We can continue on our current path and see the same results we see today. Or we can choose a different way and arouse different results.

It is crucial to utilize our skills and opportunity to teach others these critical differences to impact the future positively. Our prospects may be significant or limited to only one person, but our effort is paramount.

Norman Vincent Peale said, "One person can make a difference. You don't have to be a big shot. You don't have to have a lot of influence. You just have to have faith in your power to change things." These wise words are essential in our actions but more so in our leadership efforts because they directly affect innumerable others today and potentially beyond our lifetimes.

Robert K. Greenleaf, founder of the modern servant leadership movement said, "The servant-leader is servant first... It begins with the natural feeling that one wants to serve, to serve first. Then conscious choice brings one to aspire to lead. That person is sharply different from one who is leader first."

As with most other things, the choice is yours and mine in this and other actions daily. Time will tell the results of our response.

1 IS A MUCH LARGER
NUMBER THAN WE THINK

When we face a dauntless task, or things are not going the way we desire, it is normal to feel discouraged and incapable of changing the circumstances in our favor.

Under those conditions, many give up and walk away, sentencing themselves to endure the situation permanently.

A smaller group chooses the path less traveled and refuses to cede their desired outcome without a contest.

***

People feel overwhelmed because they don't feel able to do everything required to affect change by themselves positively. The default decision is to do nothing, but Sydney Smith warns us, "It is the saddest of all mistakes to do nothing when you can only do a little. Do what you can."

None of us can do everything in a significant endeavor, but we all can do one thing. And, we must do so.

Years ago, I took off work and spoke against a bond election at the Austin City Council. I was the lone voice in the chamber that day but was too energized in my opposition to realize at the time.

When I left the chamber, people who agreed with my position but had not spoken up publicly swarmed me. I found myself thrust into the leadership position for the campaign against the bond package. Our group was underfunded and against all of the media and city leaders.

Upon completion of counting the votes, we won in a true David vs. Goliath fashion. It proved when one person steps out as an example; others will follow and act. If enough people act, there is an exponential compounding effect in the result.

***

Another habit that thwarts action is waiting for "all" of the information before proceeding. This habit creates what some identify as "analysis paralysis." It's easier to rationalize inaction because all decision points aren't known.

As I tell people, there are those who look for reasons to make things happen and others who look for reasons not to make things happen. I'm part of the former group and biased toward others in that camp also. Anyone can make up an excuse for inaction.

In 1898, Lt. Colonel Theodore Roosevelt was the executive officer with the Rough Riders in Cuba. Troops constantly complained about a lack of resources to delay action. Roosevelt, who was well-known to be a man of action, told them in no uncertain terms, "do what you can, with what you have, where you are at." Pushed, pulled, and denied excuse by Roosevelt, they swarmed and conquered San Juan Hill in the most famous battle of the Spanish-American War.

While an ambitious man, even Roosevelt couldn't envision the overpowering popularity of that victory, which eventually delivered him into the White House as the 26th president of the United States.

When in doubt, action is always better than inaction.

***

Finally, we must always expend our best effort regardless how daunting the task is. We won't always succeed when we act, but we will consistently achieve more than with inaction. And, we will also always learn valuable lessons that will benefit our future efforts.

Who knows what lessons learned from a failure propel us to unimaginable success in the future?

In the 1970s, courts suspended the death penalty for a period in the United States. Juries in northern Texas were famous for handing down mind-boggling sentences to ensure criminals wouldn't see the light of day and threaten the citizens.

In one case, a jury convicted a man for killing a law enforcement officer. The jury handed down an 800-year sentence. Before being taken away to the state prison, the judge asked the fellow if he would like to make a statement.

Sheepishly, the man stated, "Judge, I don't know if I can serve 800 years."

The judge casually replied, "That's all right, son, just do the best you can."

That is all any of us can do. If we're fortunate, we'll have at least one experience that confirms the importance of always giving our best effort in every endeavor.

***

In early 1940, Germany had gobbled up most of Western Europe, and conventional wisdom believed they would conquer England quickly. Once accomplished, the remaining allies would sue for peace, and Germany would be free to prepare to pursue its unquenchable ambitions.

In the *Darkest Hour* in time and in the movie portraying the time, Winston Churchill became Prime Minister in the United Kingdom in May 1940. Opposing politicians fought him, and ambitious members of his party preached a negotiated surrender mediated by Italy as the only logical decision to preserve England.

Churchill rightly calculated the cost of going down swinging to be similar to voluntarily surrendering. He told his cabinet, "The nations which went down fighting rose again, but those which surrendered tamely were finished." He also realized a minuscule possibility to endure until the United States entered the war and increased the odds of victory.

Unlike most politicians whose paramount interests were in their careers, British citizens vigorously opposed capitulation to the Germans. Their determination emboldened Churchill.

After his war cabinet meeting on May 28, Churchill stood up in Parliament and declared Great Britain would fight and **"let it end only when each one of us lies choking in his blood upon the ground."** While many dark days lay ahead, negotiating a peaceful surrender wasn't again considered.

Churchill's single-handed resoluteness stopped defeatist attitudes dead in their tracks. His strong confidence lifted the Allies until they secured victory. His demonstration of what is possible from one person's determination should encourage us to always stand up to whatever obstacles and discouragement and to NEVER QUIT!

***

What are the Three Steps We Must Take When Facing Obstacles?
1. We can't do everything, but we can all do at least one thing.
2. We must act and not delay waiting for complete information.
3. We must expend our best effort always until we win or lose.

The Benefits of Competition and The Lost Art of Sportsmanship

Where did it go wrong?

The balance of healthy competition utilized for personal development and building sportsmanship extended to enhance personal relationships has been significantly damaged in the past few generations.

**

Competition is a beneficial exercise building physical, mental, emotional, and spiritual muscles to serve us when faced with future challenges. It burns zero calories, contains no harmful ingredients, and produces all-natural benefits.

Athletic contests are a tremendous outlet for competitive spirits and deter applying those physical energies into war and conflict. When war unfortunately arrives, those sharpened by winning and losing in other disciplines have an advantage over others with less experience. They are more confident, resilient, persistent, and relentless to exert themselves until victory or defeat, and thereby enhance their country's national security.

The benefits of competition are not limited to athletics but extend to nearly every area in life, not prohibited by do-gooders looking to prevent hurt feelings. Business, music, dancing, singing, cheerleading, spelling, cooking, card games, and dominoes are but a few other examples of contests offering more to participants than a bit of fun.

Today, we either have no competition or fight to total victory in unimportant contests. Grace and kindness in victory have given way to embarrassing and demeaning the victims. Losers often pout, sulk, and whine, claiming the victors stole the match from them or victim status.

While on the surface not keeping score and de-emphasizing competition defers heartaches from losing, they are a tremendous disservice to people in the long term. While altruists may control some contests, they cannot control the global competition in life where the competitive outcomes determine liberty, self-sufficiency, and sovereignty.

Sentimentalists believe they protect people from pain, but in reality, they only defer the pain and life lessons until an individual faces an unavoidable contest. Deferred lessons only exacerbate the suffering once reality replaces the false security the individual previously experienced.

***

None of us experience victory in every competition or even every time. Therefore, even the best competitors realize a loss, and sometimes often.

Baseball, as an example, is a game of failure. Hall of Fame players averaged only about three hits for every ten at-bats during their careers. Dealing with and overcoming repeated setbacks is an essential part of success in the sport.

Baseball Hall of Fame member Yogi Berra famously quipped, "Baseball is 90% mental. The other half is physical." While humorous, he was most accurate in the indispensable requirement of conquering the mental challenges of failure in achieving success.

Defeat requires us to get back up off the ground and get back into the contest to overcome the setback and attain victory. There is no disgrace in failing, only in not striving to achieve our very best self.

We only lose when we quit, as we forgo the opportunity to overcome our loss and achieve victory.

***

Good sportsmanship used to be a badge proudly worn after contests by both winners and losers.

Today, honorableness is not only forgotten, but poor sportsmanship is reinforced with celebration. My first recollection occurred when Muhammad Ali stood over Sonny Liston after knocking him out in a 1965 title rematch. It was the first but not last caption to an image stating, "in your face."

Billy "White Shoes" Johnson of the Houston Oilers introduced the first post-touchdown dance in the NFL. What startled fans then as a self-centered demonstration today looks very tame compared to current antics.

Former Texas Longhorn football coach Darrell Royal used to tell his players when they scored to "act like you've been there before" and flip the ball back to the referee. I believe our quiet confidence can intimidate others with less demonstration than a hollow boisterous display of emotion with little behind it.

The last refuge of good sportsmanship today is found in golf. Rarely do players show emotion, and it is found most often in frustration with a poor shot. On a rare occasion, players reveal their true competitive spirit celebrating a great shot or victory. More importantly, it is almost unheard of seeing or hearing a player demean another player on or off the course. They remain the best example for young people of how to conduct themselves in competition.

***

Ideals from the Olympic games of amateur athletic competitions used to measure your personal capabilities against others to pursue maximum individual performance has degenerated into overpaid professionals using the event to bolster future earnings through sport, endorsements, and other uses of their "brand."

The founder of the modern Olympic Games, Baron de Coubertin, said, "The most important thing in the Olympic

Games is not to win but to take part, just as the most important thing in life is not the triumph but the struggle. The essential thing is not to have conquered but to have fought well."

The games resumed in 1896 for amateur athletics. Rules were strict about competitors receiving remuneration for their performance. Jim Thorpe was stripped of his two Gold medals in 1912 because he played in **one** minor-league professional baseball game for $2.

Today, the games are full of professional athletes, and no one discusses or wants to remember the true spirit of the event. As in so many other areas of life, money has triumphed over principle.

***

Famed sportswriter Grantland Rice wisely observed, "When One Great Scorer comes to write against your name, He marks, not that you won or lost, but how you played the game."

Yes, all of us who have competed in any arena, athletics or otherwise, have felt the sting of defeat. Sometimes it fades more quickly than others.

Regardless of how long we nurse our losses, most of us would agree we learned more from the defeats than our most significant victories. Both are necessary to build successful people, organizations, and countries.

***

How can our actions return healthy competition and good sportsmanship?
1. Embrace the benefits of competition despite its occasional pain.
2. Proactively work to sharpen competitive skills.
3. Display good sportsmanship in victory and defeat.
4. Be good examples to others, especially the younger generation.
5. Teach others the long-term values of competition and sportsmanship.

6. Return the proper perspective of competition and sportsmanship to all contests.

7. Enjoy your experiences, realizing none of us can always win at everything.

Is the Busyness of
Life Beneficial or Detrimental?

We go and go and go some more. If you discovered this issue previously, you plan personal and family time proactively, so you don't look back and wonder why you spent all of your time working.

We have more conveniences than ever and are more productive than ever, but at what cost?

***

Nearly all of us recognize the symptoms, but very few have succeeded in re-establishing a work-personal balance in life.

Our calendars are constantly full. We have difficulty squeezing in activities we believe are essential and commonly overschedule trying to "have it all" like the fictional movie and television characters we observe.

We're always busy but never seem to gain any ground toward achieving our goals and dreams. We're exhausted at the end of each day, but it doesn't appear we accomplished anything worthwhile when we look at our day's activities.

We feel out of control and believe our activities are controlling us. We're not alone, as many find themselves experiencing this phenomenon.

We grasp short-term successes to validate our efforts that don't contribute to our long-term goals. Consequently, we compound our frustration of seeing no progress in life.

We continually multi-task with the futile hope to get ahead of our daily requirements. And, we succumb to the 24/7 pressure to instantly respond to every communication and demand others put upon us, hoping to hear words of appreciation validating our efforts.

***

Our family, health, social, spiritual, and work lives pay a severe price when we're out of balance.

We sacrifice our relationships with inattention weakening them. When we need them in the future, we'll discover the actual cost, which will adversely affect our future.

Our interpersonal skills may suffer if we overlook their importance and fail to practice them regularly. It has been said often and deserves often repeating that electronic communications are no substitute for face-to-face conversations.

If we're out of balance distracted with too much leisure and pleasure, we'll suffer long-term financial challenges. How often do we see individuals who spent their early years playing with no disregard for the time beyond their prime earning years? The opposite effect is just as bad when someone works and saves but can't take advantage of it because of years of neglect in their personal life. Stated differently, one spends too much time on unimportant matters and too little on things of great importance.

***

If you identify with the statements above, your next question is, what can I do before it is too late? Below is a simple list of actions we can all do to improve our efforts and our life results. **We can Overcome wasting time and missing opportunities by taking these steps:**

1. **We should take quiet time regularly to reflect, really listen for the Spirit, and respond to the inspiration we receive with action.**

   According to John Mark Comer in *The Ruthless Elimination of Hurry*, our busyness, which he describes as the "noise of the world," blocks our ability to hear God speaking to us. Only when we retreat into silence will we receive that voice clearly. Failure to listen to that paramount voice damages us more than all the other activities in our busy lives.

2. **Set annual life goals, and review and revise them regularly through the year.**

3. **Setting goals in six categories will improve our balance because we won't find ourselves living unbalanced lives in only a few areas.** Sections include, but feel free to add or modify:
   - Faith
   - Family
   - Personal
   - Professional
   - Physical
   - Social

4. **We should prioritize our activities based on their contribution to our goals.**

   One great way to make saying "No" easier to minimize distractions is to turn down opportunities that don't contribute to our annual goals. It is much easier to say, "I would like to consider your request, but it doesn't fit into my goals this year" than to merely say, "No, thank you."

5. **We should make sure to "act" at every stage in life!**
   - Learning isn't only for our school years, but the most successful people historically are **"lifelong" learners.**

      They self-educate far beyond whatever formal education they experienced, and their constant quest for knowledge propels them past those who less actively add to their understanding.
   - We should **transfer our knowledge and experience to others by assuming leadership opportunities**.

Opportunities appear differently for every individual, but once opened, they will continue for the rest of our lives.

Leadership is a force multiplier because it expands the possibility of our impact through those we inspire and motivate to action.

- Lastly, we each have an opportunity to impact people beyond our lives by **leaving a legacy**.

Some never think of this possibility, and others recognize it too late to maximize their impact.

My suggestion is we should think, right now, of what benefit our knowledge and experience might be to others. Even if it only of interest to our descendants, we should capture it. I wish I had more information about what my forefathers believed, thought, and any life advice that might smooth my path.

6. **We should all live the "long game."**
    - Notable author Stephen Covey suggested we look at the end of our lives and visualize how we want others to see us.
    - If we act every day to achieve that reputation at our passing, we will achieve it or come closer than if we don't set our sights on that objective.
    - This focus provides us an additional opportunity to say "No" to requests that don't contribute to our desire to finish in life.

7. **We should all strive to be the very best examples during and beyond our lives.**

None of us have a choice in whether we are an example or not. We're all examples to someone and often many. Entertainers and athletes beg people not to look at them as examples to enable behavior without guilt. They and others often learn too late being an example is not a choice.

Each of us can be the best example we possibly can be by acting daily in a way worthy of others emulating. A simple but effective rule is if you wouldn't want your grandmother to discover what you did, don't do it.

If we stop, reflect, think, rebalance, and proceed with the six steps above, we will live more stress-free, productive, and enjoyable lives. In doing so, we can maximize the benefits of life's busyness and minimalize its detrimental effects.

It's always too soon to procrastinate, but it's never too late to start and act.

Yes, There Are Life-Altering Differences Between Any Autocracy and Republic

While people may appear indistinguishable on television and in the movies, their unseen souls render their lives vastly different. Theoretically, a benevolent autocracy ensures people are equal in treatment and result.

Unfortunately, we don't live in a theoretical world, but one governed by age-old human nature, including greed, envy, jealousy, and vain ambitions. In the words of the immortal philosopher Yogi Berra, "In theory, there is no difference in theory and practice. In practice, there is."

***

Idealistic organizing principles for communities and nations have existed since time began. Monarchies, dictatorships, communes, and other forms are launched with the grand fanfare that, "this time it will be different because those who went before us weren't as smart as we are."

Enough people are mesmerized by the hope of the ultimate utopia, and they support the structural change that results in a much worse condition than the one they sacrificed.

***

When will people realize human nature is the same today, as in the beginning, and will be the same thousands of years from now? If we accept that principle, we can learn from past failures and improve on the few successes to elongate their survival.

When we look at the results of autocratic vs. republican forms of government, the choice for our life becomes much more manageable. Gone is the emotional rhetoric, media disinformation, and false narrative "this time will be different."

Cemented into our consciousness is the realization that the only organizing structure providing individual liberty and freedom is a representative republic. Yes, republics have consistently failed over time, as have autocracies.

The difference is republics fail because corruption replaces the lofty principles that founded them. Autocracies fall because people eventually rise up and demand a better life and treatment from their government.

***

Autocracies sell themselves as existing "for the people" with inspirational slogans emphasizing the "collective" and "equality for all." In reality, it is impossible for equality in result to ever occur in humankind for so many reasons that no one can assign blame.

Some people work harder than others, invest more time in their education, prioritize facets of their life differently, have more positive attitudes, are more relentless in their efforts, and many more attributes. People also have been born with different talents from their Creator. Yes, some people begin with an advantage from their parents, the location of their birth, and inherent gifts. But it has been demonstrated endlessly over time that individuals beginning life with less have succeeded because of their efforts.

Republics don't sell equality but opportunity and liberty to pursue our dreams to the best of our abilities. The validity of this position is easily proven by merely spending time with other people. Some have more talent than I do in certain areas, and I have more talent than they do in other areas. Our individual personalities and character shape the expenditure of energy toward our goals. Additionally, our skills and efforts ebb and asymmetrically flow during our lifetimes. Some people start fast and peak early, and others success is concealed until later in life when it skyrockets to infinite heights.

Willow trees grow two or more feet per year but top out around thirty feet or so, while magnolia trees grow very slowly but grow to sixty or eighty feet and beyond. **In life, it's not where we start but where we finish that counts.** Our activity in life has significantly more impact on where we finish than what we possessed when we began! We care more about our dreams and results than any government or collective! If it happens, it is up to me to make it so!

In reality, republics are the actual government form "for the people." They permit individuals to retain their liberty and power willingly rather than seizing it in the name of the greater good.

***

In exchange for the promise of equal results in life, security, and reduced risk from the vagaries of life, autocracies demand subjection, dependence, and compulsory participation. Too late, people realize the error of their ways. Extricating themselves from the trap is much more demanding and costly than entering it initially.

Benjamin Franklin knew a little about subjection to autocracy and a republic. He wisely said, "Any society that would give up a little liberty to gain a little security will deserve neither and lose both."

Our forefathers paid a dear price to gift us the liberty and responsibility connected in a republican government. Millions more from that time to the present have sacrificed to preserve it, and many more have contributed to the building of our country and becoming a "more perfect union," as stated in the U.S. Constitution.

Through the twin double blows of memory loss and entitlement, the voice of the critic of our republic speaks loudest. It has been given credibility and amplification from the fourth estate of our media.

The time for us to contribute our portion to repay the favor of the gift of liberty we have inherited is upon us. We must stand up to the threat of this generation, speak out against those spreading the seductive falsehoods of equity and security, and teach our children to value their inheritance.

***

I submit the simplified chart below comparing characteristics of autocratic and republican governments. I believe it simplifies our choice, the desire for our children and expands our appreciation of our forefathers.

Type of Government

Category	autocratic	republican
Classification	Dependent subject	Free citizen
Focus	Collective	Individual
Leadership objective	Divide and control	Unite and lead
Motivation style	Discouragement	Encouragement
Relation to government	Dependence	Independence
Involvement	Compulsory participation	Voluntary association
Result	Tyrannical oppression	Liberty and Freedom

Founding father, Samuel Adams, spoke unequivocally about the difference between patriots desiring liberty and individuals seeking security. He said, "If ye love wealth better than liberty, the tranquility of servitude better than the animating contest of freedom, go home from us in peace. We ask not your counsels or arms. Crouch down and lick the hands which feed you. May your chains set lightly upon you, and may posterity forget that ye were our countrymen."

I've lived long enough to remember when this subject wasn't in question because almost all citizens agreed on the greatness of our country and the superiority of our republican way of life. Unfortunately, those days are gone and will only reappear with our commitment, diligence, intrepidness, and relentless determination.

LEADERSHIP IS MORE THAN
BARKING ORDERS

2021 Confirmed the Lack of "Real Life" Leadership Skills of Many Politicians. Implementation messaging went from bad to worse as everyone who wanted the COVID-19 vaccine obtained it, and the effort to convince skeptics commenced.

The longer the campaign continued, the warier the holdouts became because of mixed and pessimistic messaging. Day by day and week by week, negativity and panic increased, and inspiring messages evaporated.

***

It finally dawned on me: this event revealed most politicians' lack of "real-life" leadership experience. Our country's founders envisioned citizens leaving their homes and work to serve the public in elected office for a few years and then returning to their private lives. This concept worked well while the amount of power and money in politics was minimal.

As the government expanded, it transferred more authority and capital from private hands to the public under the premise of providing for the greater good of the taxpayers. A class of people appeared who made government their business and career. Upon completion of their formal education, they latched onto a public position and sometimes only left feet first on a gurney.

Simultaneously, a class of professional bureaucrats and lobbyists arose. With the professional elected officials, these groups worked feverishly to create a perception that government work was too complicated for citizens, and John/Jane Q. Public should entrust it to the career "ruling" class. Lawyers discovered they were more adept at winning this game than most other professionals. One of the earliest buyers of this messaging was the media, who reinforce the perception to access the glow of political power and money.

This progression results in elected officials, bureaucrats, lobbyists, and media with minimal outside experience in the real-world lives of the people they purport to serve. The consequence is that each group serves themselves and each other but rarely serves their constituents because they don't know them, their interests, or their needs.

In most operations, while everything is running smoothly, the quality of leadership isn't as important. Feckless leaders can serve undetected in good times, but when adversity strikes, their incompetence exponentially magnifies the damage incurred.

When the fur of adversity flies, competent leadership is essential!

***

Individuals whose only leadership experience is in positions from which they can dictate people to obey their every order rarely understand or know how to lead individuals who don't have to follow every command barked at them. They rarely implement the steps below because they believe the people they rule only need to obey the order of the moment.

Former Dallas Cowboys coach Tom Landry defined leadership as "is getting someone to do what they don't want to do, to achieve what they want to achieve." No athlete wants to pay the price to become a champion, but every athlete wants to be a champion.

It is the same in most other endeavors; people rarely utilize their talents or push themselves to achieve their best destinies. If they are fortunate, they encounter at least one capable leader who sees more in them than they see in themselves.

Influential leaders inspire people to scale heights they didn't dream possible. Every step in their ascent affirms their effort, increases their confidence, and motivates them to pursue their very best every day.

***

Effective Leaders
- Have a vision
- Create a plan
- Communicate their proposal
- Inspire their team to achieve the project
- Lead the team from the front in executing the strategy
- Adjust the program based on resistance and obstacles
- Achieve the goal and celebrate success

***

Motivating Techniques Include

Carrots		*Sticks*
Business	**Nonprofit/Volunteer**	
Money	No $$$	Do it because I told you to
Job security	No job security	Micromanagement (breeds contempt)
	Recognition	Do it or else
	Empower (builds loyalty)	We'll come door to-door and make you
	Make a Difference	Propaganda
	Personal Growth	Beatings will continue till morale improves
	Learn for future	
	Part of Team	
	Contribute to a grand mission	
	Legacy	

***

Notice above that under business, I list only money and job security. Many of the leaders I encountered in the corporate world used these two items as carrots and sticks, and they were the only techniques they relied upon.

The very best leadership training I experienced was leading nonprofit and volunteer organizations. Money and job security are unavailable motivators in that atmosphere. Success depended on learning why people joined the team, creating techniques to inspire them individually, and incentivizing them to become valuable team members and pull them behind me instead of pushing them.

To this day, I can spot a veteran volunteer leader in a company as they employ those same valuable tactics in leading their business. They are usually head and shoulders above leaders without that arsenal of techniques. I can't encourage everyone enough to volunteer, step up in a leadership role, and learn about people and what motivates them to sacrifice their time, talent, and treasure as volunteers. When we implement various tools with the team and others based on individual motivations, our success grows exponentially. Learning those lessons may be the best business training you ever encounter!

***

One of my favorite leaders was Sam Houston. After the Alamo fell on March 6, 1836, Houston led the army and citizens on a six-week trek across southern Texas toward present-day Houston. It is known as "The Runaway Scrape" as Santa Anna's army was in hot pursuit.

Nearly everyone had lost someone in the revolution. Texans were infuriated with Santa Anna executing all prisoners, including 400 at Goliad and an unknown number at the Alamo. Instead of running, they wanted to turn and exact revenge for their loved ones on their enemy.

Houston recognized Texas would have one shot at victory and independence and could win only if his leadership controlled the people and selected the best time and place to attack. Day after day, soldiers and officers petitioned Houston to turn and fight. Those 46 days were fraught with peril, and only Houston's reputation enabled him to restrain the army. The slightest hiccup and everything could unravel dooming independence.

On April 21, 1836, Houston turned his troops and overwhelmed the Mexican in an immortal eighteen-minute fight securing Texas Independence. "Remember the Alamo" and "Remember Goliad" were the battle cries that elevated the Texans to victory!

I believe it is one of the greatest and most underappreciated examples of successful leadership in history. Houston would not have succeeded only barking orders without positive inspiration and a reservoir of credibility built over time.

***

President Ronald Reagan inspired Americans that they could achieve more and be more. Reagan delivered his message at a time when the people of the United States were disheartened, and it lifted the people's spirits. A decade of innovation, prosperity, and peace transpired because individuals realized they could pursue their dreams freely. Instead of their government demeaning them, their esteem and self-worth increased because the president encouraged them to succeed. In doing so, it was one of Reagan's significant contributions to the success of the country.

President John F. Kennedy, in his inaugural address on January 20, 1961, set people's expectations stating, "Ask not what your country can do for you, ask what you can do for your country." He established a national goal to land Americans on the moon within the decade. We achieved an ambitious goal, though he didn't live to see it. He inspired the country and each person to dream big, aim high, work hard, and persist in the face of obstacles to achieve greatness. We seldom hear rhetoric like that from elected leaders today.

***

Today, politicians sound desperate, like bad guys ready to knock over a liquor store for cash.

Many elected "leaders" demonstrate they ONLY know how to use the stick as a motivator because they have no REAL-WORLD leadership experience. They are used to DICTATING orders to people who can't say NO.

Leaders with real-life experience know negative motivation only works in the short-term and creates residual negativism toward the leader.

Real leaders inspire ordinary people to do extraordinary things, bring different people together as a united team, and focus on the next generation, not the next election.

Our best hope for leaders with the experience to inspire, and motivate citizens, is to discourage career politicians by reducing pay and benefits, rotate bureaucrats between multiple agencies to defuse their power, and restrict lobbyists' access and activities. Suppose we can return to a day with citizen representation in elective, administrative, and advocacy groups instead of careerists. In that case, we will realize better results from people who recognize it may next be our turn to represent them.

WHEN DID LEADERSHIP TURN INTO ORGANIZING, AND WHAT DOES IT MEAN?

I'm old enough to remember when people respected leaders for their accomplishments despite their shortcomings. I remember when we celebrated individuals for taking responsibility for leading groups and achieving goals. "If your actions inspire others to dream more, learn more, do more, and become more, you are a leader." —John Quincy Adams

Rewards and increased responsibility showered successful leaders, and those who fell short picked themselves up and applied lessons learned in new opportunities. Most people feel proud and respected when they are called a **leader.**

For thousands of years, people have studied leadership and improved upon it to build today's society. Untold books, speeches, and development courses communicate leadership techniques and secrets to new generations ever wanting to reach loftier goals.

And yet, despite these endeavors, a new descriptor is displacing leadership, and though appearing interchangeable, nudges society in a different direction.

***

What is the word more universally used in place of a leader in recent years? It is **an organizer.** Historically, people thought of organizers more narrowly with efforts to institute unions in organizations.

I first encountered an "organizer" when I found myself leading one side in a city bond election in 1987. The organizer was a full-blown Saul Alinsky protégé. Preparing for campaign combat, I read *Rules for Radicals, Reveille for Radicals,* and every magazine article about Alinsky I could locate. Since our opponents published their strategy and tactics, it was easier to frame the debate and win the election. Most of the United States learned of Alinsky via Hillary Clinton and Barack Obama, who exercised the organizer playbook.

More recently, when organizations publicize activities and media mention them, nameless organizers are often referred to instead of leaders. Maybe I'm overly sensitive, as I cannot find any recognition or concern toward this trend.

***

www.socialworkdegreeguide.com offers an article titled ***5 Functions of a Community Organizer*** on its website. On the surface, it is easy to overlook the overlapping aspects of organizing and leading. The differences interest me, and are worthy of noting.

Unique organizer "duties" as commonly defined by Social Work Degree Guide include:

1. work with the people of the community and not for them.
2. role of community organizer is advisory rather than direct leadership.
3. develops leaders among the community members, grooming them to become the face and the voice of the community.
4. community organizer plays an important role in developing, assessing and changing social policy as it relates to specific groups.
5. work alongside the group, guiding their efforts through direct or indirect intervention, and the group effects changes

In laymen's terms, organizers work within our social system to change it leading from behind. By serving in an advisory capacity, and not working for a community, organizers avoid the responsibility leaders accept with their duties.

***

A simple comparison is instructive for us. When Americans declared independence against England in 1776, it wasn't to overturn the social order but to change government's form, location, and representation to its citizens. We have been blessed with more than 200 years of success and individual liberty, although in a nonlinear progression.

On the other hand, French citizens stormed the Bastille in 1789 to overthrow the monarchy and establish a new social order and a monumental political shift.

According to https://franceglobalissues.weebly.com, France has had 11 government regimes since 1789 compared to one for the United States and The United Kingdom. Though it started as a people's revolution, the succession of governments resulted in increased government power and reduced citizen liberty.

In my opinion, the lesson is equity, and social justice movements usually result in more government and less individual freedom despite their idealistic objectives. Would Americans be happier with that outcome or prefer incremental improvements of our established and successful system?

***

Free enterprise economics best serves free people with proven leadership principles that reinforce economic and political individual freedom. Adam Smith's "invisible hand" theory advocated individuals making free choices will result in greater wealth for all than a planned and controlled economy. His most famous work, *An Inquiry into the Nature and Causes of The Wealth of Nations* in 1776, was studied by our nation's founders and has repeatedly been proven since first advocated.

***

Seven Principles Successful Leaders Employ to Reinforce Social Norms and Positively Impact the Present and Future

1. Leaders **accept responsibility** for measurable action by election or appointment. They are identifiable to their team as the leader.
2. Successful leaders **visualize where they want to take an organization** and communicate it to their followers or constituents.
3. Successful leaders **realize long-term success beyond their tenure is best for the organization and team members.**
4. Leaders **inspire others to follow them**, sacrifice other time, talent, and treasure opportunities, and commit themselves to give whatever is necessary to achieve the common goal.
5. Leaders **motivate their team to persevere through adversity** and overcome all challenges.
6. Successful leaders **train their teams** for increased responsibility and leadership opportunities. They also **prepare their successors**, ensuring the continuity of organizational success.
7. Exceptional leaders **cherish the opportunity to reward team members whose valiant efforts contribute to team success.**

The next time you hear the word "organizer," see if there is more to the organization than achieving its stated objectives. An additional consideration is especially true if you are considering joining its efforts.

Why are Some Leaders Oblivious to Their Negative Examples?

When will corporate CEOs learn their every action is under the microscope resulting in disproportionate impact, whether good or bad?

Not since I wrote about **Radio Shack** laying off 400 employees by email in 2006 has a more tone-deaf personnel action occurred than the one by Better.com CEO Vishal Garg in December 2021 and March 2022.

***

Radio Shack was paradise for the DIY electronic enthusiast. My dad was a huge fan. Peaking at about 7,000 stores often found in small strip centers in 1999, it was the go-to store for electronic products and parts. By 2021, they are a shell of their former glory, with about 500 franchised stores through further mismanagement.

While not the only misstep example in the decline of a great company, laying off 400 employees by email caused more damage than leadership anticipated. Every business school and leadership training program should study Radio Shack's example of how not to act.

As excerpted from *Conquering Life's Course: Common Sense in Chaotic Times*, I wrote:

"Do you think any of those individuals released will speak positively of the company or continue to be customers?

"While management's act was impersonal to the individuals directly affected, I was astonished because company leaders obviously didn't think about the impact on those remaining employees. Did leadership believe that their decision was made in a vacuum? Do executives believe the people who survived the layoff will be happy or even more anxious about when and how they may be let go? Will the company have any credibility with its employees when they communicate about the state of their business?

"At a time when **Radio Shack** needed everyone to contribute their best effort and demonstrate the highest team spirit, management revealed an extreme case of expediency and cost-control over caring about the feelings of loyal employees. Management will state that their action reduced expenses by a certain amount, but they may never know how much it cost them in the future because of their insensitive action. I contend that the short-term expense of conducting the layoff more humanly would be far less than the long-term cost of their decision."

Years later, we see Radio Shack not only didn't rebound from the insensitive move, but they have also continued to suffer a further decline. Our following example illustrates a failure to learn from this example and commit an even more egregious act if you can believe that.

***

December 2021 gave us a more outrageous example of poor executive management when Better.com CEO Vishal Garg fired 900 employees during a Zoom call. His complete lack of empathy toward those affected surprised me since he had previously similarly terminated employees. That makes the offense and lack of learning a valuable lesson even more breathtaking.

Adjusting personnel for market changes is understandable,

but terminating a large group via video call is impersonal, and it included belittling language and ignored the company's recent cash infusion. The CEO's negativity on the call displayed his typical management style of punishing people over minuscule errors and using negative language to motivate increased employee productivity.

Within a few days, three executives resigned from Better. com. They publicly spoke against the CEO's leadership style in another sign of a poorly run organization. They accused him of not listening to anyone, believing his ideas were always correct, not accepting any advice.

Shortly after the layoff call, the CEO gathered the rest of the company. He told them they should have instituted the layoffs three months before. I doubt he wondered during his presentation what the remaining employees were thinking. His message slamming the employees' departed colleagues further illustrated a complete tone-deafness to human nature in general and his associates specifically. My bet is they, like their Radio Shack predecessors, wondered if they were next and when, and as the old adage states, "beatings will continue until morale improves."

A couple of days later, the CEO issued a tail-between-his-legs apology via email, which of course, leaked almost immediately. Revealing a company's confidential communication further illustrates the negative attitude among employees.

I'm sure the associates read the apologetic tone in the message and wondered if it was sincere or merely a forced eyewash to save his job and please investors. I'm sure it will be many months before employees believe his statement based on his leadership style history. To regain any trust from his team, he will have to actually change completely into an effective leader who knows how to inspire workers to achieve higher performance.

Better.com was poised to issue a public offering during the fourth quarter of 2021 but had to push the launch back due to the blowback from the layoff debacle. The cost of that decision could more than offset any personnel cost savings from the layoff. I'm thankful not to be an investor in Better.com with leadership like that. I would wager the CEO will leave before the public offering is re-attempted and efforts to resell the business and elevate stock values are completed. Again, time is money, and delay negatively affects money.

Just when you thought an executive or company couldn't be more insensitive in how they handled employee layoffs, Better. com proved us wrong. Instead of utilizing Zoom to communicate the layoff of around 3,000 in March of 2022, employees learned of their dismissal via an on-line deposit of a severance check.

Executives scrambled to reverse the premature transactions, but the damage was done. The reason for the action wasn't important, but another bungled execution is cause to question management's competence.

***

What are the easy, practical lessons we can learn from these three events?

1. **Experience matters.** More-tenured leaders would have known about Radio Shack and not repeated it.

2. **We must learn from our mistakes.** The CEO had conducted a similar layoff previously but did not learn from it.

3. **How one terminates, an employee is as important as the decision to do so itself.** Losing one's job is a life-changing event. Goodwill is essential to every business, and no company benefits when former employees speak negatively about their experience.

4. Most employees are conscientious and want to perform well. **Positive motivators are much more effective in achieving company goals than negative ones.**

5. **From entry-level to CEO, teamwork means every employee deserves equal respect and consideration.** Better.com's CEO exhibited a complete disregard for all of his associates and acted from a place of superiority. No employee responds well to narcissistic leadership.

6. **Confident leaders hire executives better than they are and listen to their advice.** No one knows enough to make every decision without executive input. The Better.com example illustrates that insecure leaders look to demonstrate their mental superiority at every opportunity, which the Better.com example shows.

7. **Leadership selection for boards of directors and investors is critical.** Too often, businesses overlook the soft interpersonal skills for technical, finance, or other complex skills. A leader's ability to inspire and lead people is the most crucial skill set required for success. It is easy to find technical leaders, but effectively leading people is a more elusive yet critical requirement.

Real Leaders Respond Rationally to Challenges, Not Emotionally!

When things are going well, leadership is no trouble. As I often say, the most crucial management decision is knowing when to stay out of the way. Easy times obscure leaders' shortcomings, successes outweigh failures, and observers focus on good news instead of negativity.

When challenging times arrive, they reveal everyone's true capabilities. They magnify leaders' performances because of their exponential influence on more significant responsibilities. Poor decisions result in defeats, which build upon themselves until units spiral out of control. Team members recognize leaders pushing them to increased failures.

It is pretty standard for poor leaders to become excessively emotional when their blemishes are exposed for all to see. Their reactionary responses appear out of control and can create panic. They often assign responsibility for failures before gathering facts, which demonstrates inferior decision skills. When they throw their team members under the bus, it demoralizes the entire team.

***

Successful leaders' contributions to organizational success are taken for granted when things are going well. Successful leaders create more good times than bad, with effective leadership further conditioning people to assume achievements occur because they always have before.

When lean times do arrive, usually brought on by influences outside the control of an outstanding leader, responses are rational and productive, mitigating adversity's impact.

When others are frustrated and out of control from challenges, exceptional leaders maintain a calm appearance.

They retain control of the organization, which reassures all constituents that they will ride out the trouble in the smoothest conditions. They defer decisions until they consider as many facts as possible to make the best long-term decisions. And, they give their team members the benefit of the doubt in personnel matters, enhancing trust in the leader.

***

Joshua Chamberlain was a professor and theologian by profession. In July 1863, he found himself a Lieutenant Colonel and the executive officer of the 20th Maine Regiment in Gettysburg, Pennsylvania. His unit was very active July 1 and was assigned the left flank of the Union line on Little Round Top on July 2 to rest.

Superiors ordered Chamberlain to protect the left flank of the Union line at "all costs" if an unforeseen attack occurred.

The afternoon of July 2 found Alabama troops attacking Little Round Top attempting to flank Union troops. Repeatedly the rebels attacked and were repelled by Union troops. They constantly moved to the right compelling Chamberlain to move his forces leftward to maintain the army's line.

Chamberlain's junior officers counseled retreat or surrender with little ammunition, many wounded and dead, and fatigue hampering his defense. Chamberlain knew those choices were unacceptable, and the consequences could influence the entire war, the 1864 election, and America's future.

During the height of tension and confusion, Chamberlain shouted the one order no one in either army expected. "Charge," Chamberlain shouted, urging his troops down the hill to the surprised look of the Alabamians.

Union soldiers swept the field in a few moments, and the threat was over. Chamberlain's leadership earned him lifetime respect from his soldiers, Robert E. Lee's sword at the Appomattox Courthouse surrender on April 9, 1865, and four terms as the governor of Maine. His leadership and choice in a moment impacted the ages.

***

When challenges arrive, successful leaders:
- Acknowledge the news
- Retain control and appear calm
- Investigate facts promptly and completely
- Determine appropriate response
- Consider **precedent** decision will make
- Consider **example** their action and decision will set
- Inform team members ahead of the public privately if punishment is involved.
- Communicate decisions openly and decisively
- Enforce appropriate action
- Modify organization for future success

Leadership is the difference in any organization's crucial moments. Prominent organizations invest the effort and pay the price, filling critical positions in anticipation of lean times. Organizations surviving and succeeding decades and longer illustrate the benefits of remarkable generalship.

LEARNING, LEADING, AND LEGACY

"What you leave behind is not what is engraved on stone monuments but what is woven into the lives of others."

—Pericles

"The man who only speaks to one generation is already dead. And he who listens to only one generation is deaf."

—William Spence in the movie *One Foot in Heaven*

What Difference will it Make 100 Years from Now?

What difference will your actions today make 100 years from now?

If I heard Bill Battle, my dad, say that once, I heard him say it a thousand times. It usually accompanied him eating something that wasn't healthy for him or some other pretty innocent activity. It was his way of enjoying the present without any negative impact on the action in question.

Until long after his passing, I not only didn't think deeply about the statement but used it myself.

Then a revelation made me see the expression in an entirely new light.

While it is still correct that eating something outside of our diet will not make any difference in the world 100 years from now, other endeavors will shift the future.

The world and time are great distractors. They seduce us to focus on now, with little regard to the future, and on instant gratification without consequence. The world and time seem so significant that they discourage us from believing that we can have any effect on either one of them.

The world whispers the big lies to eat, drink and be merry for tomorrow we die and what happens in Las Vegas stays in Las Vegas. Matthew, Mark, and Luke ask us, "What does it profit a man to gain the whole world, and yet lose his soul?"

Time seems to stand still when we're waiting for something that we want to happen. But, blink twice, and twenty or more years will have seemed to have flown by us. The phenomenon of time passing faster as we age is so common that scientists study it. Dr. Haddon Robinson said, "Time is our enemy disguised as our friend." We each get twenty-four hours a day, but we don't receive the same number of days. It is paramount to maximize the impact of our time "under the sun," as the book of Ecclesiastes instructs us.

I have been as guilty as anyone in abusing time and falling for the fake of the present. A lot of my previous efforts served the present and the world, but not the world of 100 years from now.

***

In reality, 100 years from now is critical in our decisions for then and our daily lives. And, it is crucial in our ability to influence the future on this earth and beyond.

Our touch 100 years from now will result significantly from our interaction with those we directly relate with and indirectly influence through various activities.

Our impact may come through significant actions or seemingly inconsequential moments. They may be things that we'll know when they occur and remember, or we have no idea of their occurring until someone acknowledges it to us in the future. Or, we may never see the total of our impact on the future.

***

My great-grandmother passed when I was 9. She would be 152 now. Her teaching from my great-great-grandmother to her, my grandmother, mother, me, and my daughter spans almost two centuries. I have my great-great-grandmother's table where she served cookies to my teenaged great-grandmother's guests and the guest book autographed from 1884. They are tangible reminders of the continuity of our past, present, and future generations.

When we administer life lessons, it is easy to focus on the present or near-term future. In reality, when we instruct our children, we provide our grandchildren and beyond training.

That makes the proactive teaching of proper values and culture the most essential leadership opportunity given each of us. How we utilize each day is more impactful than we may believe.

It is as important to teach American history, values, and exceptionalism as well. If we don't, they will be lost in the next generation.

***

I always strive to provide value to everyone I have the privilege of interfacing with, whether in a work or personal scenario. As I have gained additional insight, I have strengthened my efforts and attempted to deliver more essential nuggets that the individual may benefit from and share with others, which will magnify their impact through time and more people.

What 100 years from now looks like depends on what we do today.

I hope that you will discover the opportunity of influencing the future far earlier than I did.

There is Always One More Question, Idea, or Action that will Improve our Impact on the World

The combination of political chaos, COVID pandemic, and depressing news discourages many, including me, sometimes. The sense of futility in restoring everyday life and society can be overwhelming.

What can I do? What can any one person do to make a positive impact on this ever-increasingly destructive society?

Day after day transpires as I searched my mind and asked God what I can do to change the trajectory of this world?

Finally, it dawned on me. I was frustrated and overwhelmed because I was trying to solve all of this world's problems. I'll bet others suffer the same crushing belief.

The spirit touched me with an encouraging revelation. **None of us can do everything to change circumstances, but we can all ask one more question, think of one more idea, and act one more time to positively impact our family, work, country, or our lives.**

That is the secret. We should all search for our passion, and upon identifying it, look for the most impactful opportunity to contribute one more thing to make the difference most of us want to do in this world.

As I reveled in my realization, I recognized throughout history those who made significant differences in this world did so in varying degrees of volume. Some only made narrow but focused contributions. Others made wide and shallow impacts.

Still, others contributed widely and deeply in many areas. The key was they all did something vs. being paralyzed in inaction.

I encourage you and me to act today when others won't to achieve tomorrow what others can't. Too many people talk about doing things but never commence their actions. We should not be those people.

Right or wrong, others should see and recognize we are people of achievement. We act and do not wait past the point of maximum opportunity to move. We do not let the enormity of a challenge deter us from contributing what we can. As General George S. Patton said, "Successful generals make plans to fit circumstances but do not try to create circumstances to fit plans."

***

This principle extends into enterprises we are already actively committed to executing. We often experience a vision of something important to accomplish, develop a plan to achieve it, and implement the program to its fulfillment.

As we're completing implementation, and sometimes after the endeavor has concluded, we realize we could have done one more thing to increase the results exponentially. We make a notation for ourselves, and the next time the event is conducted.

The question we should ask ourselves early and often during the project is, "what one more thing can I do now to increase the success of this enterprise?

***

Whether we feel overwhelmed or we've done everything, there is always one more question, idea, or activity we can do to increase our positive impact on a situation.

While the statement may sound trite, I'm amazed how often my performance improves due to my straining my thinking beyond where I stand at any given moment. The feeling of satisfaction and resulting achievement from the additional ideas are often the difference between success and failure. Depending on the endeavor, it may be life-changing or life-saving.

Even if the additional effort doesn't result in improving results, it is worth the effort!

***

The late Steve Jobs, the co-founder of Apple, was famous for completing new product introductions, turning to leave the stage, and then returning to introduce an additional offering to an eager and adoring audience.

If we can use "one more thing" as a presentation tool, why shouldn't it be used at every step and every day in people's lives? His utilization of that communication technique changed the thought processes at Apple and his audiences and impacted people worldwide.

If it worked for Jobs and Apple, isn't it worth our consideration and adoption? I would advocate it is in everything we do.

***

How can we adopt the "one more…" discipline to improve our lives and the world?

We should Always:
1. **Observe everything in our surroundings.** We never know where or when an idea will appear. Think actively about improving what we're doing. The "it's always been done that way" thinking should be regularly tested and revalidated.
2. **Ask questions to ensure we know "why" we do what we do.** Finding a mentor who will counsel us is invaluable in increasing our knowledge and testing our ideas.
3. **Act! Resist analysis paralysis.** It is almost impossible to delay movement, waiting for all the information to make a perfect decision. We must act at the appropriate time to maximize the impact of our decision with the information we have in hand.

4. **Review and revise.** As we continue our efforts, lessons will appear we need to learn for our future benefit and to others observing our accomplishments.
5. **Resist criticism from armchair quarterbacks.** Rarely do people not in our shoes know all of the factors in decisions and executing plans. It is acceptable to listen for the occasional breakthrough idea but resist any negativism.
6. **Rest at the appropriate time,** confident our efforts were the best at the time with the information available.

***

Right now, where you are, and whatever you are doing, ask yourself the question below. Develop the habit of asking yourself regularly this question. Soon, it will be so natural; you won't have to think about doing it.

What is One More ... we can do today to make a difference in what we're doing?

A Splash of Hope in Uncertain Times

Yogi Berra would have been proud. It was "déjà vu all over again."

Many would agree that the only certainty in 2020 was its total uncertainty.

Americans everywhere celebrated the August 2, 2020 splashdown of the SpaceX Dragon spacecraft. It was a joyous interlude in an otherwise forgettable year.

I believe this single achievement is more meaningful than most will realize because it displayed control and success during an unpredictable and uncontrollable time. It joins December 17, 1903, June 6, 1942, and July 20, 1969, as the most important dates in aviation history and preserving our national security.

1903 saw the Wright brothers inaugurate powered air flight, which began the march to air travel we enjoy today. Adapting flight for military use is a mixed blessing but is essential for our liberty.

June 6, 1942, was the decisive encounter during the Battle of Midway, which saw the conventional wisdom of naval warfare transformed from ship-to-ship engagements to air-to-ship combat being a necessity for victory. It forever changed naval operations.

Who alive on July 20, 1969, can forget watching Apollo 11 land on the moon? To this day, hearing the replay of Neil Armstrong's first words after stepping onto the moon's surface reverberate in our souls. He said, "That's one small step for man, one giant leap for mankind." The United States continued to dominate the space race for many years until our leadership diminished our efforts as unimportant.

That brings us back to August 2, 2020, which I believe is even more critical for our future than the previous milestones. It re-energized the United States' quest for space preeminence, which will secure our future sovereignty unless we throw it away.

My experience with SpaceX began in 2015 at my initial meeting as a member of The Texas Emerging Technology Fund advisory council. The first piece of business I voted on was to approve an investment in the SpaceX company for their Boca Chica, Texas, launch facility.

While others celebrate the first "splashdown" of an American spacecraft in forty-five years, I believe three other facets of the mission are more noteworthy.

First, the United States launched a space vehicle for the first time in several years. Riding a Russian craft to space was inexcusable. It ceded our country's excellent space exploration tradition to other countries. We need to **reclaim our status as the No. 1 country in space exploration.**

There was the similarity of launch and splashdown beneath four gloriously deployed parachutes for we who grew up watching Mercury, Gemini, and Apollo. For all of us today, the utilization of technology unimaginable during earlier missions sparks our imagination for future possibilities.

Second, SpaceX demonstrated the benefits and capabilities of a private company. It completed a mission many believed only a government could accomplish. While there was governmental support, **this was free enterprise at its finest.**

Bob Behnken and Doug Hurley commanded the ship and the SpaceX team exemplified everyday Americans accomplishing extraordinary feats. After its splashdown, citizens in boats surrounding the craft added that this was a significant win for all Americans!

What other feats can private enterprises achieve in the future? The possibilities are almost as vast as the sky.

Third, when our country was divided into many fragments, **this mission was something all Americans could celebrate.**

While we have more things that unite than divide us, media attention presently overemphasizes divisive issues.

As we march toward the future, I hope we return the focus to our common cause of "forming a more perfect union." Each step will be smaller than this gigantic one but essential nonetheless.

FORGIVING OTHERS IS ONE OF THE BEST GIFTS TO OURSELVES

How can it be possible to receive more from a gift you give someone else than the person to whom you give the gift?

How can we forgive someone who has injured us physically, mentally, emotionally, or in any way?

What is the mystery that results from forgiving someone that lifts our spirits more than not forgiving them?

***

Human nature is perplexing sometimes. Our natural tendency is to dislike or hold an even angrier attitude toward people who wrong us. For some reason, we feel our negative response will harm them when in reality, it rarely disturbs the person because they didn't care about us before they injured us.

Grudges and feuds sometimes lasting generations occur because the aggrieved party believes it will hurt their enemy. Again, in reality, the harmed party is most often injured a second time from their bitterness.

***

I've written previously about my experience investing in income-producing real estate. The first seven years went well, and I was on my way to achieving financial security. Out of the blue, the U.S. Congress changed the tax law, and the real estate market nosedived within ninety days.

Month after month, for what seemed like an eternity, I had to withdraw hard-earned savings to cover additional expenses. Finding tenants became more complicated, and collecting rent was even more challenging. I had one tenant from whom I had to collect rent weekly after returning from my business travel. Tenants destroyed property, looted appliances, and caused other damage because they perceived I was a rich landlord.

When I finally found a purchaser for one property, he collected rent but never made a mortgage payment. It compelled me to foreclose on his agreement and return the property to my portfolio.

The experienced seemed like it would never end, but it did after three years. It left me with a choice. Did I hate those who abused me, look for vengeance, and retain a bitter attitude?

Thankfully, I knew any negative feelings I might hold wouldn't harm those I held responsible for my circumstance. I flushed my negative thoughts and chalked them up as a costly and painful education. Doing so enabled me to look forward to the future instead of back into the past. The future held promise, opportunity, and optimism, whereas the past had only negative thoughts and feelings.

***

Matthew 6:15 teaches us "but if you do not **forgive** others their sins, your Father will not **forgive** your sins." While I was familiar with the Scripture in theory, my real estate experience tested me and converted it to experiential knowledge.

Forgiving someone who harms us once is difficult enough. How can we forgive someone who repeatedly abuses us? Yes, it strains our ability to overcome our human nature.

But we hope our Heavenly Father forgives us over and over during our lifetime. He expects us to do likewise. Luke 17:4 tells us "Even, if they sin against you seven times in a day and seven times come back to you saying 'I repent,' you must **forgive** them." Understand, I have not mastered nor will I master this command, but I hope and believe I am better than before. Additionally, I hope to mature and learn from others' examples, whichwill enable me to grow better at forgiveness.

***

Charles Larkam and I had been good friends who had shared enough experiences to develop a deep bond when tragedy struck his family in 1986.

His father was managing an apartment, which he also used to positively impact the residents' earthly and spiritual lives. Late on a Sunday night, a tenant insisted he go to the apartment he and his brother shared to repair a water leak. When he entered the bathroom, the brother struck him eleven times with an 18-inch lead pipe, killing him. It was a senseless crime committed against a man who only tried to help the person who deprived him and his family of the remainder of his life.

Charles's initial response was a realistic option. He left town the next weekend and traveled to Dallas, Texas.

On that Sunday, Charles and his brother John were attending a church service. Charles was overcome by his feelings and left the sanctuary for the foyer in mid-service. John and one of his friends joined Charles to pray with him. They convinced Charles of God's love and provision and persuaded him to be baptized in the Spirit then.

On Charles's return drive to Austin that evening, he prayed for direction and received the presence of God in a way that changed his life. In addition to confirming his faith, he decided to forgive the two brothers that night.

A few months later, the two brothers' sister called Charles to apologize on her family's behalf. She asked Charles if he would speak by phone to the brother who committed the murder as he sat in jail.

The initial phone call turned into several in-person visits over time where Charles demonstrated forgiveness and communicated the blessings he received from his faith and forgiving the criminal.

For we who were friends of Charles, his example was monumental. If he could forgive the men who murdered his father, couldn't we forgive people who committed less severe infractions against us? Charles's model of Christian behavior helped all of us to grow and become better people.

Charles continues to share God's love and the gift of forgiveness with others. His actions have and will touch an untold number of beneficiaries. His positive response to a horrible event adds impact to his dad's shortened life that otherwise may not have occurred. We don't know the Lord's plans for us, but if we respond to our life events correctly, we'll fulfill His purpose for us.

Additionally, if we obey God's command to forgive others, we will live freely indeed!

***

Charles R. Swindoll tells each of us, "Life is 10% what happens to you, and 90% how you react to it." Our choices not only affect our future life but those who harmed us and all we encounter in the future.

Will we remain bitter, live in the past, and drive others from us with our anger and hatred? Or, will we discard our fury after a grieving period, forgive those who hurt us, learn the lessons from experience, and proceed into the future with hope and optimism?

The choice is always ours, and the future we realize will result from our choices more than any other factor.

***

My desire is we all discover when we forgive others, we are giving the best gift to ourselves.

Wouldn't It Be Nice?

As we fantasize about a different ending to 2020 than the sudden and monumental life changes we realized in March, it reminds me of the old Beach Boys song, "Wouldn't It Be Nice." It focuses on teenage love, but its wishful wail also applies elsewhere in life.

***

We can wish about the return to the pre-pandemic status and resuming the quest for our unachieved dreams. The one I want to focus on is the degradation of etiquette in the world of politics.

It wasn't too long ago society restrained the world of politics in a narrow slice of our lives. We could easily escape it with sports, entertainment, our faith, and many other areas. Unfortunately, those days are long gone, and politics invades every institution in life.

***

Not since the 1850s has our country been as divided about its future as we are now. The political discourse at that time led to the Civil War, which killed more Americans than any other war we have endured. Political civility eventually returned. Leaders realized without a more peaceful and civil discussion of the day's crucial issues our civilization would disintegrate.

Principled representatives from every area of the country holding all the facets of the matters discussed helped keep personal differences out of the debates. Our country succeeded as never before, and the respected peaceful transfer of power from one party to another became the hallmark of our nation's stability.

The athletic metaphor from that period occurred in 1865 when the 9th Marquess of Queensberry endorsed the civilized rules of boxing, which are the basis for the modern sport. The regulations resulted in a spirited competition without the bloodlust seen before their adoption.

Today's athletic metaphor would be the Ultimate Fighting Championships or The Texas Cage Match from where I grew up. The rules in these events seem to be anything goes except for murder. That pretty well describes the level of political combat in our country today.

***

If we retain our place as the world's superpower and dominant culture, we must restore the civil political debate in our country. Others may see me as naïve, but our forefathers restored civility for those of you who still study history. There is no valid reason we can't achieve the same results unless we fail to change. Yes, both sides have to change, or the effort will be doomed to failure.

I believe there are seven achievable attributes to return our political dialogue to civility and ensure our future success. They are:

1. We must limit our speech to the issues and refrain from personal attacks.
2. We must speak civilly and refrain from personal hostility emanating from our speech.
3. We must demonstrate maturity in responding to the other side instead of immaturity.
4. We must restore common sense responses to events rather than emotional reactions.
5. We must believe and communicate our principles and avoid moral relativism.

6. We must place country, state, and city over personal power.

7. We must be an example as statesmen instead of displaying ambition and the quest for personal power.

Will a return to civil political discourse be easy? No. Will it be without failures along the way? No. Will both sides err in the effort? Yes.

Is the effort worthwhile? Absolutely!!!

People of all beliefs must step forward and step up in this effort!

It is The Right thing to do for the long-term health of our country and ourselves.

***

The concluding verse of "Wouldn't It Be Nice" by The Beach Boys applies to young love and the return of civility to the political discourse.

You know it seems the more we talk about it
It only makes it worse to live without it
But let's talk about it
Oh, wouldn't it be nice?

WHERE DO WE GO FROM HERE?
DO WE RE-ESTABLISH FREEDOM OR
COMPLETE THE NANNY STATE TRANSITION?

Have you felt it yet?

Every day, government intrudes more and more into our lives. In every action, they snatch from us a piece of our liberty, most likely gone forever.

I'm old enough to remember the fresh breath of freedom to choose. Yes, with liberty comes risk and sometimes failure and pain. But there is no more incredible feeling than to exercise independence and realize an achievement because we had the opportunity to reach beyond our grasp to improve our lives.

***

Our founders were skeptical of government power, which time bears out repeatedly since our country began its uneven ascent to prosperity. Religious, political, and economic liberty inspired countless individuals to strive toward their dreams. In doing so, they collectively built the most prosperous country in history and demonstrated western civilization's values, which provided individual natural rights and responsibilities as free citizens.

***

Rugged individualism produced strong men and women, but the ever-increasing reliance on government has transformed many into weaklings today.

My parents, grandparents, and great-grandparents relied on family, friends, neighbors, and the church during tough times. The government was the rescuer of absolutely last resort. Today, governments promote being the rescuer of the first choice, which depletes our strength individually and as a country.

Our freedom is like a muscle. When we don't exercise our responsibilities, we become weak. When we lose our strength as citizens, we lose our rights and become subjects to whatever tyranny has seized power.

***

Life is too complicated and challenging to exercise individual freedom, you say? I say poppycock!

People perform in any setting to the level leaders expect them to perform. If we raise standards and expect higher levels of performance, people will respond and achieve it. Leaders demanding excellence successfully validated this maxim for almost two hundred years.

Recently, it became in vogue to lower standards to allow more people to qualify in many systems. If we lower standards in the name of fairness, performance levels will fall to creep over the low bar of achievement. Lowered standards producing reduced results also has been proven repeatedly, though it isn't politically correct to point this out to anyone.

The result is lower levels of performance by individuals and our entire society. When we observe beneath the surface other countries, which are more "progressive" than the United States, this theory is proven. The incentive for everyone to exist at the same level of mediocrity is in every institution.

In addition to lower physical performance levels, people's spirits become crushed because they are limited to their "station" in life, with an almost nonexistent opportunity to escape via their exceptional performance in any endeavor.

***

In some countries, nanny states arrive via a revolution to "save the people," which results in tyranny. In other societies, totalitarian rule creeps in one step at a time.

The diversion of pleasure and personal interests is seductive. Citizens discard responsibility and deferred gratification, thinking they can retain their freedom along with more fun and less responsibility. Unfortunately, the real world doesn't work that way.

***

To remain free, we must resist the siren call of a government that wants to "take care of us." "A government is like a fire, a handy servant, but a dangerous master." –President George Washington

***

Our freedom necessitates us spreading government power to the lowest level, involving more people in decisions, and holding those responsible directly accountable to local citizens.

As citizens, we must regularly exercise our oversight so "public servants" are reminded every day that they work for the citizens and not the citizens for them.

People who expect any president to issue a decree to give them a specific result will soon find that same president issuing commands they abhor.

***

Government overreach is not a partisan issue as politicians on both sides of the aisle are prone to increase their power. Although, there is one party that is much more aggressive and adept at it than the other.

Our founders' brilliance of understanding human nature's eternal consistency in exercising power inspired them to create a unique structure to protect our liberty. They designed a government with three branches, separated power, provided checks and balances, and confirmed states retaining power not expressly delegated to the federal government.

Citizens retained power not delegated to government and enumerated individual citizens' rights to protect us from the government are unique features of our republic.

Our republic has survived 234 years but is weaker than ever and under a more significant direct and indirect attack than ever before.

***

No one conceived of limiting elected officials' terms at the founding because no one believed anyone could sacrifice their livelihoods for government service as a career.

After President Franklin Roosevelt's precedent-breaking election for four terms, Congress passes, and states ratified the twenty-second amendment limiting presidents to two terms.

Congress to date has not sacrificed their privilege of unlimited terms resulting in too many of them only leaving feet first. Career officials limit the number of people who can serve, limit ideas, become entitled to their position, sometimes pass their job to relatives as if they were in the monarchy, and lose the perspective of who is the boss and who is the servant in the country.

Elected officials spending decades in office believe in more and more government and less freedom for citizens. If we are ever to return the proper emphasis on those elected serving the people, we must enact term-limits for all elected offices throughout the land.

***

What can we do to re-establish and expand our liberty?

1. Stop expecting the government to provide anything outside its enumerated powers at all levels.
2. Share your concern about losing your liberty with others to sound the alarm.
3. Relax. None of us can do everything. Find your passion and apply it to one thing and make a difference!
4. Vote freedom first! It requires more diligence to identify candidates who talk big but don't protect liberty. It is worth the effort!
5. Encourage your leaders to reclaim your state's rightful power from Washington. Let them know you know their responsibility.
6. Hold schools accountable for their materials and teaching methods to ensure students learn our rich heritage, proudly live as Americans, and mature into the next generation to protect freedom.
7. Be an example to others as you excel in the pursuit of your dreams and achievements. Your success will inspire others to reach beyond themselves. Individual independence is a threat to nanny-state governance.

Pursuing individual dreams creates national greatness through Adam Smith's invisible hand, while pursuing collectivist dreams creates servants only to the elite rulers!

We, the people, get the freedom we demand and earn. When we surrender our independence, we get the government only too happy to dictate everything in our lives.

Is There Any Difference in Being a Slave to Man or Government?

Historically since the earliest of times, part of the population was slaves to men. While slavery still exists in 2021, the United States uniquely fought a war ending in 1865 to abolish it, costing more than 600,000 lives.

Though uneven, the efforts to "form a more perfect union" stated in the Constitution continue today.

Now, we all risk becoming slaves to a government by giving up our freedom in the pursuit of equality of outcomes. Our forefathers saw themselves enslaved to a monarchy. They wanted to be free and fought a declared war for five years to win their liberty. Thankfully, subsequent generations have each continued to pay whatever price was required to preserve our gift of freedom.

Those two events made me think about the difference between being enslaved by man or by a government?

It may seem like a distinction without a difference, but I disagree.

***

When some are free and others are slaves , as before 1865, injustice was institutionalized. While not free, freedom could be seen and hoped for by those enslaved.

Since 1865, all citizens are technically free, but most would agree there has been an unequal application of freedom. Again, some experienced partial freedom and hoped for total freedom they viewed but did not realize.

Slaves to men are totally subject to the rules and whims of one man or organization. Some owners are brutal tyrants whose slaves experience the very worst of life. Other owners treated their slaves better but did not grant them their freedom. Both alternatives were appalling, but one was worse than the other one.

Slave markets existed where people were bought and sold, and families split apart at the pleasure of those who benefitted from owning people. It isn't easy to imagine this occurring in our history and to this day elsewhere.

***

While enslavement to man is horrific, I believe enslavement to government is far worse. The primary reason is that everyone except a few officials is in the same position with virtually no hope of improving their status during their lifetime.

The form of government is not the predictor of enslavement but the individual's position in relation to that regime. Monarchies, dictatorships, religious autocracies, and even facades that appear as democracies exist as soul-stealing and hope-crushing states.

The common denominator is the subjection of the individual to the collective of the state. Some create the illusion of equality of the population, and others don't pretend individuals have any value other than sacrificing their lives for the "greater good" of the government.

There is no motivation to pursue excellence with extraordinary exertion for those countries where people believe equality will occur. If people think outcomes will be the same, why invest any exercise into the same result regardless of effort? The product is societal stagnation and the death of individual creativity, which benefits everyone.

***

Individual liberty is seldom discussed by politicians in our country anymore. It used to be celebrated by both political parties, and now it is exclusively mentioned only occasionally by one party. who recognize the unique gift bestowed upon us of individual freedom are frightened, knowing it is not paramount to all who desire to lead us.

There is no liberty when the government pursues equity as it proactively manipulates results in a vain attempt to achieve equality of outcomes. And, there is no individual liberty without economic and political freedom.

Our freedoms have decreased substantially during my lifetime. Things I freely enjoyed are viewed with amazement or incredulity today by those who haven't and can't experience them for themselves. Students who drove pickup trucks to high school regularly carried guns in gun racks for use on their farm or ranch. No one thought anything of it. Today, arrest awaits any student arriving at school with a weapon.

At young ages, we had the run of our neighborhoods and town to explore as we wished. Today, parents would forfeit parental rights for allowing children such freedom. If we had the cash, we could buy products such as glue without signing documents or having our parents present.

Civil and criminal statutes exist as created by the people's will as the guardrails of civil society but can be prostituted to enact and enforce tyranny.

President Ronald Reagan was a great advocate and protector of liberty who wisely said during his farewell address in 1989, "As government expands, liberty contracts." Unfortunately, he continues to be proven right over and over during our lives.

Stifled dreams, lost hope, and aimless futures result from organized government authoritarianism. In this way, there is no difference between being a slave to a man or a government.

***

As I waited to speak to a service representative regarding maintenance for my truck, I noticed and then focused on a single bird flying in the area. He or she effortlessly glided or furiously flapped its wings, flew higher in the sky, or dove toward the ground and changed from working for food to playfully enjoying its trip. Watching this one bird provided me unpaid entertainment and eased the time as I waited my turn in line.

Then, I begin to think about the freedom that bird enjoyed I had enjoyed in full measure previously and less so currently. That is one advantage and disadvantage of being a mature adult. We know more about what we had and lost than those younger who never knew the levels of freedom our forefathers and we possessed.

Think I'm wrong? My new bird friend flew where it wanted, how it wanted, when it desired, why it chose, for what purpose it craved, and with or without whom it wanted to associate. Americans used to have all of those freedoms!

Some of them perished even before my arrival, but the pace of loss has accelerated rapidly more recently. The shocking realization is how easily my fellow citizens relinquish choices to a national government they primarily made or were overseen by a local authority.

Freedom is not only a state of existence and an American right, it is a muscle that we must regularly exercise to strengthen for the tough times we all face in life. The more of us who wield authority over our lives not only build us up but reinforce our community and nation against all threats, foreign and domestic. Conversely, ceding power to third parties weakens us individually and corporately.

I wrote previously about a friend who returned from a military assignment in Europe. When I spoke of the excessive regulation code enforcement implemented in my community, he laughed. He told me of an experience where a friend went to work, and when he returned, he discovered local authorities had painted his house and placed a bill in his mailbox. It was all courtesy of the local authorities who deemed the painting necessary. The home occupant had no choice to paint the house or even the color but only to pay the bill or reap more authoritarian rule.

If Americans don't exercise freedom, this and much worse mastery of our lives will arrive. It doesn't matter if an authoritarian is a leftist or rightist, as they all seize all of the power allowed by the public. Catastrophe comes when freedom vanishes because it is much more difficult to wrestle it back from an oppressive government than win initially. Our forefathers sacrificed greatly to present us this gift of immeasurable value.

***

Slavery to anyone or anything is unacceptable. Preserving our freedom and passing it on to future generations is paramount.

The next time you spy a lone bird majestically soaring in the sky, celebrate its liberty, and exercise yours!

OUR FOUNDING PATRIOTS BLESSED US GREATER THAN OUR APPRECIATION OF THEM

In a rush to destroy our history, we often overlook the brilliant men who crafted our Declaration of Independence with logic and reason rather than emotion and anger. In 1776, God aligned the stars and happened to bring 56 men who represented all Americans.

They realized as soon as they signed their names on the Declaration, they committed themselves fully, and there was no turning back to the old order of life. They risked "their lives, fortunes, and sacred honor" to fight a protracted war of independence and create a republic that has stood for 245 years.

These were serious men who knew what they risked and why but felt the gamble was worthwhile to create a unique place on earth where men governed themselves and individual liberty was the order of the day.

As told in *The Lives of the Signers of the Declaration of Independence* by B. J. Lossing, nine died fighting, or from hardship, twelve had their homes pillaged and destroyed by the British, five were captured and tortured before dying, two lost sons, another had two sons captured, and others lost wives and fortunes.

Their commitment, dedication, persistence, resilience, resolve, and relentless pursuit of creating a country where people would be masters of the regime instead of slaves to it lasted almost seven years.

Selected quotes from the leaders still apply today, illustrating the consistency of human nature and the relevance then, today, and tomorrow of the Declaration of Independence and subsequent Constitution as our guiding documents. Their love of country and recognition of its exceptionalism is worthy of our emulation.

***

"My only regret is I have but one life to give for my country."
—*Nathan Hale*

"Give me liberty or give me death."

—*Patrick Henry*

"I am not certain if I can; At least I'll gladly try. Your country's flag behold!"

—*Betsy Ross*

"It is impossible to rightly govern a nation without God and *The Bible*."

—*President George Washington*

"We hold these truths to be self-evident, that all men are created equal, that they are endowed by their Creator with certain unalienable Rights, that among these are Life, Liberty and the pursuit of Happiness."

—*President Thomas Jefferson*

"Liberty once lost, is lost forever."

—*President John Adams*

"If men were angels, no government would be necessary. In framing a government which is to be administered by men over men, the great difficulty lies in this: you must first enable the government to control the governed, and in the next place oblige it to control itself."

—*President James Madison*

"The greatest tyrannies are always perpetrated in the name of the noblest causes."

—*Thomas Paine*

"I have not yet begun to fight."

—*John Paul Jones*

"No matter what you do, you'll never run away from you."

—*Paul Revere*

"It is in the interest of tyrants to reduce the people to ignorance and vice. For they cannot live in any country where virtue and knowledge prevail.

—*Samuel Adams*

"If ever a time should come, when vain and aspiring men shall possess the highest seats in Government, our country will stand in need of its experienced patriots to prevent its ruin."

—*Samuel Adams*

***

These men were not perfect but were brilliant because they recognized man's imperfection, including in themselves. They also distrusted government, realizing its tendency to evolve into a bureaucratic master if citizens surrendered their independence.

They sacrificed monumentally to give us individual liberty with political and economic freedom. Those twin freedoms are inextricably intertwined. We either preserve both or lose both; that is our responsibility.

***

In 1787, 55 men gathered in Philadelphia intent on modifying or replacing The Articles of Confederation, which delegates ratified in 1781. Thirty-nine of them plus the convention secretary signed The United States Constitution, a brand-new document, which is now the longest active governing document globally.

Again, reason, deliberation, prayer, and crafting the best ideas from around the world entrusted ultimate power to the people, then to the states, and lastly to a limited federal authority. They recognized they didn't give us a perfect government but one they hoped the people would continue to "form a more perfect union."

***

The founding patriots of the United States from the Boston Massacre in 1770 through the Constitutional Convention correctly understood the inherent nature of humans. The relevancy of their thoughts and writings confirms the immutable agelessness of human nature and reaffirms the brilliance contained in the Constitution and Declaration of Independence. The Constitution is not a breathing document that follows changes in human development but is a solid foundation constraining the worst tendencies of humans to enslave people through government because human nature has not, nor will not, change.

Succeeding generations of our forefathers faithfully preserved the gift and passed it along. Now, it is our turn to execute our responsibility to sustain our individual liberty and mastery over our public servants.

If we honor our founders and predecessors, we'll breathe our last breath as a free person, confident we repaid the favor given to us.

If we fail to stand up to the forces intent on subjugating all people to the rule of man instead of the rule of law, we will enter darkness long before we take our last breath. Those following us will be sentenced to only long for the freedom we enjoyed, for as President John Adams said, "Liberty once lost is lost forever."

***

Every day and in every action, we make choices contributing to our future freedom or eventual subjection. It is up to each of us to contribute to the freedom of future generations rather than squander our inheritance.

Is the Material World All We Need?

The material world distracts and leads us only to death, while the spiritual world is seen only by discerning eyes yet leads to eternal victory.

Yes, we all need material things to live: food, water, shelter, clothes, and many other items. I'm referring to an almost worship of material things to the disregard of non-material focus and thought. We should consider where we stand and whether we are happy for the remainder of Life in that position or a change is beneficial?

***

In the material world, we are incentivized to live, for now, guilted by our past shortcomings and discouraged from pursuing our dreams and taking advantage of future opportunities.

This view leads us to decisions without considering past experiences of others and the wisdom of the ages, which is available at our fingertips almost instantaneously.

The material world promotes discontinuing the pursuit of the desires of our heart because of its discouraging messages yet encourages our focus on material acquisition for satisfaction.

In the short term, Materialism can dominate our lives, but long term, a spirit-filled life is more rewarding. The material world is finite, while the spiritual world is infinite.

Do we join negative conventional wisdom or navigate our individual journey?

I believe **Materialism is our adversary camouflaged as our ally.**

***

We think the bogeyman is unseen, and the things we see provide our safety. But unfortunately, the reality is just the opposite. There is no such thing as the bogeyman, but we are constantly tested with appeals to all of our senses, leading us astray.

Media-driven consumerism appeals to our eyes and awakens our desire for more in the hope it will make us happy. Seeing things we don't have arouses our insecurity and sparks envy and jealousy within us.

Our natural response is to acquire the promoted items, which only satisfy momentarily like a child's enthusiasm for a new toy on Christmas morning. And like the child, we quickly lose interest and discard the item forgetting forever the adrenaline rush it created.

One of the tremendous examples is the home remodeling business. Television shows display supposedly happy, successful people because of their sparkling homes. The message and appeal of these shows are primarily directed to ladies, playing on their instinctive desire to nest.

The adage "if it's not broke, don't fix it" is abandoned, replacing perfectly wonderful items with those "in style" at the moment. No one wastes a breath considering how quickly the current style will pass, and the necessity to update again will appear. I've even seen people buy brand-new homes and renovate them before moving in. I wonder why they didn't build a custom home in the first place?

Before the success of the free enterprise system created current levels of disposable income, people who survived the Great Depression were much more prudent with their spending decisions. I tell people home remodeling for both of my grandmothers was a mop and a broom. Anything beyond painting when it was one step before unavoidable was extremely rare. And no one in my family suffered for it.

***

As I have said before, **Life is full of mysteries. There are things seen that drive us crazy and things unseen that give us peace we can entrust for our eternity.**

We can't see the air we breathe or gravity keeping us from floating into space, but we trust their consistency, enabling us to live in peace. We can't see so many of the essential things that make our lives more enjoyable also.

Trust is something earned over time but can be stronger than the strongest steel on the planet. **Contentment, happiness,** and **joy** can't be seen or bought but are worth more than all the chests of treasure in the world. **Hope** fuels people to risk their today, sacrifice their possessions, and move mountains for themselves and their families to deliver a better tomorrow. And **love** is no doubt the strongest unseen feeling and motivating action of them all. All history is full of stories of achievements by people because of their intense love for others. As the scripture in Matthew tells us, "Greater love has no man than to lay down his life for his fellow man."

We have a grander hope than one limited to our physical existence for those of us with faith in a life beyond this world. Our faith provides us a **purpose** above ourselves and makes our efforts in Life small pieces in a glorious design beyond our comprehension.

World War II concentration camp survivor Corrie ten Boom lived a faith tested life, experiencing depths most of us can not understand. She said, "faith sees the invisible, believes the unbelievable, and receives the impossible." That statement rings true because of her life experience not its theoretical delivery in a college classroom.

***

As we live day by day, we constantly face decisions and choices. The material world says forget yesterday and tomorrow, and live for today. The spiritual world, especially the faith-based one, admonishes us to consider the wisdom of those who went before us, the future impact of our choice on ourselves and others, and our example for the future.

If the material world is correct and there is nothing beyond this Life and Materialism, we will cede momentary pleasures living in a faith-based spiritual world.

However, if truth rewards our faith and spirit-led lives, our short-lived sacrifice will be minuscule compared to the eternal prize we receive.

Each of us chooses who to align with during Life. Which one is friend and which one foe? Materialism or the spirit?

As Corrie ten Boom also said, "The first step on the way to victory is to recognize the enemy." Her experience validated by countless others over time convicted me that our enemy is the love and devotion to Materialism.

I encourage you to stop, reflect, and make your informed decision for the future.

OUR DESTINY IS?

My late friend, J. Terryl Bechtol, profoundly stated, "Most people are too busy making a living to make a life." Little did I know how enlightened his comment was at the time.

Time, the business of life, and hindsight have elevated the wisdom in Terryl's statement, which now is a regular consideration of my decisions and activities.

I hope you will reap the value of these words earlier and the enhancement of your life.

***

Our successes and failures delivered us to our present situation and can be used to achieve an impactful future. Each of us blessed to see a new day is faced with how we will use our gift.

Too often, I have looked back on a day and realized I let it slip away with no visible progress. Other times, I look back later and recognize progress I did not know had occurred. On the best days, I retire amazed at the gifts of progress presented to me.

***

Today, the question for us is, where will I be a year from today? Five years from today? At the end of my life?

Will I progress to fulfill my purpose and serve others more than today?

We can't become the people we are destined to be if we remain the people we used to be. We must advance daily to meet the destiny awaiting us.

William Jennings Bryan said it this way, "Destiny is not a matter of chance; it is a matter of choice. It is not a thing to be waited for; it is a thing to be achieved."

Every day and every choice propels us toward our end. Most of us will leave this life without accomplishing all of our desires. Will we look back on more failures or regrets? Will we reach beyond our grasp attempting new heights or resign ourselves to the comfort of where we presently reside?

Time has reinforced my statement in *The Four-Letter Word that Builds Character* in 2006: "What you do in the present will create a past that greatly influences your opportunities and dreams in the future."

We can't achieve our paramount future today, but we can contribute a small piece toward it. But we can ruin grand moments with a misstep resulting in lost future opportunities.

***

Like most individual things in life, you can't win anything at the start or in the middle of the course. But you can lose small and large matters out of the gate with a single misstep.

The key is to set the destination and focus on the daily or individual details. Focusing constantly on the destination adds and builds pressure to achieve the goal and increases the likelihood of interim failure resulting in missing the target.

In World War II, as an example, everyone desired to achieve total victory. Every day, individuals contributed their effort to build a weapon, transport the supplies, and perform thousands of other tasks before soldiers, sailors, marines, and members of the Coast Guard fired shots to win that day. Everyone knew doing their job today was important and doing so would conclude in final victory. Everyone knew failure to exercise their responsibility could result in disaster also.

No one shot wins a match in golf, but one errant shot can lead to a loss. Every good shot builds a winning score, and the player that completes the contest in the fewest total strokes wins. This truth applies in other sports and life activities equally as well.

Champions and those achieving their highest possible destiny perform consistently, relentlessly overcoming adversity, and persistently until their time expires.

***

As we continue our journey toward life's fulfillment, our choice is, do we share the ride schooling from our predecessors, learning from mentors, collaborating with colleagues, and receiving encouragement from friends and family? Or, do we keep our own counsel and proceed for better or worse?

For we secure in our faith in the Creator of life, our purpose, counsel with the Spirit, and choices reflect a higher mission. It is true regardless of our achievements. We realize results aren't as crucial as utilizing our unique gifts to complete the plan prepared for us.

We understand all of our experiences, good and bad, prepare us for future accomplishments. It is all and always about HIM and for the benefit of others. We rely on the wisdom of Proverbs 19:21, "Many are the **plans** in a person's heart, but it is the Lord's purpose that prevails."

Where we are is nowhere near as important as where we finish. When our life ends, we long to say the exact words as the Apostle Paul in 2 Timothy 4:7, "I have fought the good fight, I have finished the race, I have kept the faith."

I believe **what we are today is God's gift to us. What we become will be our gift to God.**

***

Our question and opportunity are, what will we do from this point to accomplish our purpose and bask in the exhilaration of success? We should:

1. **Recognize** regardless of where we are, every day we are gifted, life is an opportunity to grasp.
2. **Forget** prior setbacks, so they don't hobble us from advancing.

3. **Inventory** our gifts and strengths, so we don't waste time pursuing opportunities we possess no skills.

4. **Retreat** into a quiet space (regularly) to listen for the Spirit's direction. It is amazing what we discover when we stop and listen to the very best advice available.

5. **Collaborate** with family, friends, and colleagues. The give and take of sharing ideas ripples over time exponentially benefitting people beyond our vision and time.

6. **Review and revise** progress, goals, and opportunities regularly. Avoid distractions leading to rabbit trails that don't contribute to our mission.

7. **Enjoy the results** of our efforts, realizing our conscious efforts contributed to the long-line of advancement of humanity in history.

BIBLIOGRAPHY

Alinsky, Saul. *Rules for Radicals*. New York: Random House, 1971.

Ambrose, Stephen. *Band of Brothers*. New York: Touchstone, 1992.

Battle, Richard V. *Conquering Life's Course: Common Sense in Chaotic Times*. Denver: Outskirts Press, 2019.

Battle, Richard V. *The Four-Letter Word that Builds Character*. Austin: Volunteer Concepts, 2006.

Beach Boys, The. "Wouldn't it Be Nice," recorded 1966, track 1 on *Pet Sounds*, Capitol Records, vinyl LP.

Bevan, Louise, "Man With No Arms and Legs Completes 10 Marathons, Shares Indestructible Motto: 'If I Can'," *The Epoch Times*, November 9, 2020.

Bucknam, Robert, and Gary Ezzo. *On Becoming Babywise*. Oregon City: Multnomah Books, 1995.

www.clipartkey.com.

Comer, John Mark. *The Ruthless Elimination of Hurry. Colorado Springs: Waterbrook, 2019.*

Covey, Stephen R. *The 7 Habits of Highly Effective People*. New York: Fireside, 1989.

Darkest Hour, directed by Joe Wright (2017, Universal City, California: Focus Features, Perfect World Pictures, Working Title Films.)

http://www.dreamstime.com.

Enemy at the Gates, directed by Jean-Jacques Annaud (2001, Hollywood, California: Paramount Pictures.)

Feuer, Will, "Better.com CEO Fires 900 Employees on Zoom call, accuses them of 'stealing.' *New York Post*, December 6, 2021. Follow-up articles on December 7-8, 2021.

http://www.dictionary.com/.

https://franceglobalissues.weebly.com/progression-of-government-regimes.html.

The Holy Bible, New International Version, www.biblegateway.com.

https://www.iconscout.com.

https://www.inspiringquotes.us/.

Jenkins, Dan. *Semi-Tough.* New York: Signet, 1972.

Lossing, B.J. *The Lives of the Signers of the Declaration of Independence.* Aledo, Texas: WallBuilder Press reprint, 1995.

McCarten, Anthony, HistoryExtra.com, October 6, 2017. Excerpt from the book below. McCarten, Anthony. *Darkest Hour: How Churchill Brought us Back from the Brink.* New York: Harper, 2017.

Merriam-Webster on-line dictionary, www.merriam-webster.com.

Paine, Thomas. *"The American Crisis, The Pennsylvania Journal,* 1776.

https://www.plantedshack.com/slowest-growing-plants/.

Rogers, David. *Waging Business Warfare.* Crossroad Press, 2014.

https://www.scholastic.com/teachers/articles/teaching-content/olympic-principles-and-traditions/.

Smith, Adam. *An Inquiry into the Nature and Causes of The Wealth of Nations.* 1776 first published.

https://www.socialworkdegreeguide.com/lists/5-functions-of-a-community-organizer/

Spence, Ewan. "Five Of The Greatest 'One More Thing...' Moments From Steve Jobs And Apple," *Forbes* magazine, October 19, 2013.

Trulock, Alice Rains. *In the Hands of Providence: Joshua Chamberlain and The American Civil War.* Chapel Hill: The University of North Carolina Press, 1992

www.youtube.com.

V for Vendetta, directed by James McTeigue (2005; Burbank, CA: Warner Bros. Pictures). http://www.vajaycee.org/jaycee-creed.html.

Williams, Beth. Prime East Forward Focus, "Poor *Leadership is the Number One Reason Your Employees Quit,"* https://www.forwardfocusinc.com/inspire-leaders/poor-leadership-is-the-number-one-reason-your-employees-quit/.

Appendix A

Made in America by AmeriCANS – Quotes

"Nothing great was ever achieved without enthusiasm."
— *Waldo Emerson*

"Life is 10% what happens to you and 90% how you react to it."
— *Charles R. Swindoll*

"Success is never final; failure is never fatal."
— *Winston Churchill*

"It is amazing what you can do when you don't know what you can't do."
— *Unknown*

"It's déjà vu all over again."
— *Yogi Berra*

"Hang tough."
— *Major Richard "Dick" Winters, Easy Company (Band of Brothers)*

"There are those that think they can and those who think they can't. They're both right."
— *Henry Ford*

"Service to humanity is the best work of life."
— *C. William Brownfield*

"It is the saddest of all mistakes to do nothing when you can only do a little. Do what you can."
— *Sydney Smith*

"One person can make a difference, and everyone should try."
—*President John F. Kennedy*

"Well, nobody said it wasn't going to be semi-tough."
—*Bill Clyde Puckett in Semi-Tough*

"All you really need is the One who promised never to leave or forsake you – the One who said, 'I am with you always.'"
—*Joni Erickson Tada*

"Deny your weakness, and you will never realize God's strength in you."
—*Joni Erickson Tada*

"The only disability is a bad attitude."
—*Dabo Swinney*

"You can't always avoid adversity. But you can always choose how you respond to it."
—*Charles F. Stanley*

"To stay ahead, you must have your next idea waiting in the wings."
—*Rosabeth Moss Kanter*

"Example is not the main thing in influencing others; it's the only thing."
—*Albert Schweitzer*

"A word of encouragement during a failure is worth more than an hour of praise after a success."
—*found in Encouragement quotes*

"All our dreams can come true if we have the courage to pursue them."
—*Walt Disney*

"Optimism is the faith that leads to achievement. Nothing can be done without hope and confidence."

—*Helen Keller*

"The best instruction is that which uses the least words sufficient for the task."

—*Maria Montessori*

"It's never too late to do the right thing."

—*Nicholas Sparks*

"If you have a problem that you can write a check to solve, you don't have a problem, but an expense."

—*Dr. Robert H. Schuller*

"When the road looks rough ahead, remember the 'Man upstairs' and the word HOPE. Hang onto both and 'tough it out.'"

—*John Wayne*

"Never put off until tomorrow what you can do today."

—*Benjamin Franklin*

"Never put off until tomorrow what you can do the day after tomorrow."

—*Mark Twain*

"Time is our enemy disguised as our friend."

—*Dr. Haddon Robinson*

"The past doesn't have a future, but you do."

—*Byrd Baggett*

"Have more than you show, speak less than you know."

—*William Shakespeare*

"You cannot get ahead while you're trying to get even."
—*Dick Armey*

"No man in the wrong can stand up against a fellow that's in the right and keeps on a-comin.'"
—*Captain Bill McDonald, Texas Ranger*

"If I can…you can too."
—*Chris Koch*

"Nothing in this world can take the place of persistence. Talent will not: nothing is more common than unsuccessful men with talent. Genius will not: unrewarded genius is almost a proverb. Education will not: the world is full of educated derelicts. Persistence and determination alone are omnipotent."
—*President Calvin Coolidge*

"Success is peace of mind, which is a direct result of self-satisfaction in knowing you made the effort to become the best of which you are capable."
—*John Wooden*

"It is our attitude at the beginning of a difficult task which, more than anything else, will affect its successful outcome."
—*William James*

"If you're going to be a champion, you must be willing to pay a greater price."
—*Bud Wilkinson*

"Dedication is the ability and determination to complete a resolution long after the mood in which it was made is gone."
—*Unknown*

"There are no great men. There are only great challenges that ordinary men are forced by circumstances to meet."
—*Admiral William F. Halsey Jr.*

"If you are depressed, you are living in the past. If you are anxious, you are living in the future. If you are at peace, you are living in the present."

—*Lao Tzu*

"If men were angels, no government would be necessary."
—*President John Adams*

"A government big enough to give you everything you want is a government big enough to take everything you have."
—*President Thomas Jefferson*

"A government is like fire, a handy servant, but a dangerous master."

—*President George Washington*

"People shouldn't be afraid of their government. Governments should be afraid of their people."
—*Alan Moore in V for Vendetta*

"Of all the tyrannies, a tyranny sincerely exercised for the good of its victims may be the most oppressive."

—*C. S. Lewis*

"I predict future happiness for Americans if they can prevent the government from wasting the labors of the people under the pretense of taking care of them."
—*President Thomas Jefferson*

"What kind of government have you given us, Dr. Franklin?" He exclaimed, "A republic if you can keep it."
—*Benjamin Franklin*

"Those who have a why to live can bear almost any how."
—*Dr. Viktor Frankl*

"There is no pit so deep that He is not deeper still."
—*Betsie ten Boom*

"To achieve all that is possible, we must attempt the impossible. To be as much as we can be, we must dream of being more."

—*Fred La Novel*

"Don't judge each day by the harvest you reap but by the seeds you plant."

—*Robert Louis Stevenson*

"Power tends to corrupt, and absolute power corrupts absolutely."

—*Lord Acton*

"To be born free is an accident; To live free is a responsibility; To die free is an obligation."

—*John Ben Shepperd*

"As government expands, liberty contracts."

—*President Ronald Reagan*

"People don't care how much you know until they know how much you care."

—*President Theodore Roosevelt*

"You can get anything you want out of life if you help enough other people get what they want."

—*Zig Ziglar*

"An honest public servant can't become rich in politics. He can only attain greatness and satisfaction by service."

—*President Harry S. Truman*

"It is amazing what you can accomplish when you don't care who gets the credit."

—*President Ronald Reagan*

"Do what you can with what you have where you're at."

—*President Theodore Roosevelt*

"One person can and does make a difference."
—*Albert Schweitzer*

"One person of integrity can make a difference."
—*Elie Wiesel*

"One person can make a difference. You don't have to be a big shot. You don't have to have a lot of influence. You just have to have faith in your power to change things."
—*Norman Vincent Peale*

"Successful generals make plans to fit circumstances but do not try to create circumstances to fit plans."
—*George S. Patton*

"The servant-leader is servant first...It begins with the natural feeling that one wants to serve, to serve first. Then conscious choice brings one to aspire to lead. That person is sharply different from one who is leader first."
—*Robert K. Greenleaf*

"Too many men dropped the best thing reaching for a better one."
—*Unknown*

"A man's mind is stretched by a new idea or sensation and never shrinks back to its former dimensions."
—*Former U.S. Supreme Court Justice Oliver Wendell Holmes*

"Hope is the mother of all men."
—*Private Conroy in the movie Halls of Montezuma*

"Mankind is ever advancing, yet man is ever the same."
—*Dr. Logan Cummings*

"The most important thing in the Olympic Games is not to win but to take part, just as the most important thing in life is not the triumph but the struggle. The essential thing is not to have conquered but to have fought well."

—*Baron de Coubertin*

"In War: Resolution; In Defeat: Defiance; In Victory: Magnanimity; In Peace: Goodwill."

—*Winston Churchill*

"When One Great Scorer comes to write against your name, He marks, not that you won or lost, but how you played the game."

—*Grantland Rice*

"Baseball is 90% mental. The other half is physical."

—*Yogi Berra*

"Our problem is not we aim too high and miss but that we aim too low and hit."

—*Aristotle*

"I may be wrong, but I'm not confused."

—*Darrell K. Royal*

"The cultivated mind is the guardian genius of democracy."

—*Mirabeau B. Lamar*

"Those who fail to learn from history are doomed to repeat it."

—*Sir Winston Churchill*

"Our greatest weakness lies in giving up. The most certain way to succeed is always to just try one more time."

—*Thomas A. Edison*

"The first step on the way to victory is to recognize the enemy."

—*Corrie ten Boom*

"Faith sees the invisible, believes the unbelievable, and receives the impossible."

—*Corrie ten Boom*

"In theory, there is no difference in theory and practice. In practice, there is."

—*Yogi Berra*

"Any society that would give up a little liberty to gain a little security will deserve neither and lose both."

—*Benjamin Franklin*

"If ye love wealth better than liberty, the tranquility of servitude better than the animating contest of freedom, go home from us in peace. We ask not your counsels or arms. Crouch down and lick the hands which feed you. May your chains set lightly upon you, and may posterity forget that ye were our countrymen."

—*Samuel Adams*

"The biggest lie in the world is a half-truth."

—*Bill Battle*

"Everybody has a plan until they get punched in the face."

—*Mike Tyson*

"The secret of success in life is to be ready when your opportunity comes."

—*Benjamin Disraeli*

"Success is when preparation and opportunity meet."

—*Bobby Unser*

"Act as if it were impossible to fail."

—*Dorothea Brande*

"Most people are too busy making a living to make a life."

—*J. Terryl Bechtol*

"Destiny is not a matter of chance; it is a matter of choice. It is not a thing to be waited for; it is a thing to be achieved."

—*William Jennings Bryan*

"Leadership is getting someone to do what they don't want to do, to achieve what they want to achieve."

—*Tom Landry*

"Ask not what your country can do for you, ask what you can do for your country."

—*President John F. Kennedy*

"Much of the social history of the Western world over the past three decades has involved replacing what worked with what sounded good."

—*Thomas Sowell*

"These are the times that try men's souls."

—*Thomas Paine*

"That we obtain too cheap we esteem too lightly. It is dearness only that gives everything its value."

—*Thomas Paine*

"Believe you can, and you're halfway there."

—*President Theodore Roosevelt*

"The hardest arithmetic to master is that which enables us to count our blessings."

—*Eric Hoffer*

"The mind, once stretched by a new idea, never returns to its original dimensions."

—*Ralph Waldo Emerson*

"Individual ambition serves the common good."

—*Adam Smith*

"The first principle in a free society is an untrammeled flow of words in an open forum."

—*Adlai Stevenson*

"In matters of style, swim with the current. In matters of principle, stand like a rock."

—*President Thomas Jefferson*

"If your actions inspire others to dream more, learn more, do more, and become more, you are a leader."

—*John Quincy Adams*

***

Some Americans have bought the sales pitch. It is possible to make everyone the same in society. They assume human nature is evolving into a state, making that possible. They ignore history illustrating human nature is the same today as the beginning and will not change in the future.

The following quote toward the end of the movie *Enemy at the Gates* from 2001 recognizes the futility of governments attempting to equalize their citizens.

Commissar Danilov: "I've been such a fool, Vassili. Man will always be a man. There is no new man. We tried so hard to create a society that was equal, where there'd be nothing to envy your neighbor. But there's always something to envy. A smile, a friendship, something you don't have and want to appropriate. In this world, even a Soviet one, there will always be rich and poor. Rich in gifts, poor in gifts. Rich in love, poor in love."

BATTLE'S BULLETS FOR AMERICANS

- A dream delayed is not a dream denied.
- Failure to step out of your comfort zone in an effort to achieve something significant puts you at 100% risk of never growing beyond where you are now.
- Choice + Chance + Change + Channel + Commitment + Consistent + Everyday Action = Champion
- Boring is good. – This doesn't refer to boredom but an absence of adversity.
- Nobody said life wouldn't be semi-tough – a corollary to Billy Clyde Puckett in *Semi-Tough*.
- Focus up and out, act, grow and repeat.
- Common sense is always in style and never goes out of season.
- Navigating change to success requires:
    o Anticipate change
    o Recognize it as early as possible
    o Adapt as quickly as possible
- It's not where we start in life that counts but where we finish.
- What we are today is God's gift to us. What we become will be our gift to God.
- When in doubt, know life is full of decisions. Make one.
- We never reach our full potential until we fail at our highest achievement. Until then: **Aim High, Work Hard, and NEVER Quit!** ®

- We should always help who we can, where we can, how we can.
- The longer our time perspective, the smaller today's problems appear. The shorter our perspective, the larger they appear.
- The pain of regret cuts deeper and lasts longer than the pain of failure.
- The only difference in can and can't is our temperament.
- None of us can do everything in public service, but we should all do at least one more thing as citizens, so we don't become subjects.
- Achievement builds confidence, and confidence leads to more success.
- We should honor and learn from the past, live and contribute in the present, and hope and prepare for the future.
- Don't let the person you are prevent you from becoming the person you're meant to be. Pursue your dreams!
- The more I know, the less I know, and that's all I know.
- Where we place our hope is as important as the attitude of hope itself!
- Regrets hurt more and last longer than failures.
- Longing for what we want in the future obscures our appreciation for what we have in the present.
- A good attitude is the starting point of every success.
- In adversity, I learned not to ask "why me" but "what now" in the hope I would only suffer once to learn my intended lesson. It has served me repeatedly and very well!
- Constitution Day! September 17, 1787, Though only a piece of paper, its ideals and the stability it has provided us by all citizens honoring it are unprecedented and priceless! Government of law is far superior to rule by men and women.
- What we do today, tomorrow, and the rest of our tomorrows is more important than what we did yesterday.
- You can't do anything positive with a negative attitude.

- The more we find to laugh about, the happier we will be.
- God brings experiences to us to teach us lessons. The question is, how many times do we need a trial to learn one lesson?
- Anyone can destroy a creation. Only a creator can build or rebuild it.
- If common sense was common, we wouldn't talk about it.
- "I did" is better than "I will."
- Forget yesterday, enjoy today, hope for tomorrow.
- While waiting for an opportunity:
  - Be Positive.
  - Be Ready.
  - Focus on what you can control.
  - Accept what you can't control.
- Truth is the first casualty in debate when the quest for power prevails over principle.
- Principle over power. Honor over ambition.
- There is NO individual liberty without political **and** economic freedom.
- When I focus on others instead of myself, my attitude is better, and my heart is appropriately positioned for service.
- Be careful how much government you desire. You may get it and more.
- Life is a series of mid-term examinations.
- I've never had a bad experience saying thank you to someone.
- Politics on an issue leads to power for a group, proceeds to money for a party, and the circle repeats endlessly. It's always about the politics, power, and money despite what we're told.
- One side will grow and win. It is up to us to make sure that we citizens maintain freedom and not succumb to slavery by an all-powerful and omnipresent government.
- Civil and criminal statutes exist as created by the people's will as the guardrails of civil society but can be prostituted to enact and enforce tyranny.

- Catastrophe comes when freedom vanishes because it is much more difficult to wrestle it back from an oppressive government than win initially.
- When in doubt, action is always better than inaction.
- There are those who look for reasons to make things happen and others who look for reasons not to make things happen.
- I can't get into the trouble I want to get into, and I can't get out of the trouble that I don't want to get into.
- Encouragement is the greatest gift we can give others, and forgiveness is the greatest gift we can give ourselves.
- The material world distracts and leads us only to death, while the spiritual world is seen only by discerning eyes yet leads to eternal victory.
- Materialism is our adversary camouflaged as our ally.
- Our quiet confidence can intimidate others with less demonstration than a hollow boisterous display of emotion with little behind it.
- We only lose when we quit, as we forgo the opportunity to overcome our loss and achieve victory.
- If hindsight is 20-20, and experience is the best teacher, why won't the people who have neither listen to the people who have both?
- It's always too soon to procrastinate, but it's never too late to start and act.
- Life is full of mysteries. There are things seen that drive us crazy and things unseen that give us peace we can entrust for our eternity.
- Dreams are marvelous but worthless unless we dare to pursue them!
- Until we step forward in action, victory is impossible regardless of our attitude, positioning, and preparation.
- We can't become the person we are destined to be if we remain the person we used to be.
- We must advance daily to meet the destiny awaiting us.
- What we do in the present will create a past that will greatly influence our opportunities and dreams in the

future. From *The Four-Letter Word that Builds Character* in 2006.

- Common sense isn't woke, and woke isn't common sense.
- When the fur of adversity flies, competent leadership is essential.
- Real leaders inspire ordinary people to do extraordinary things, bring different people together as a united team, and focus on the next generation, not the next election.
- There is no your truth or my truth. There is only the truth.
- Hope is always welcome and devastating when absent.
- I follow inspiration on a journey, unaware of its path but knowing its destination.
- It doesn't matter where we are today. It only matters where we are tomorrow and what we do to get there.
- Thomas Fuller said, "it is always darkest before the dawn."
  - o We're also:
    - Most lost before we find our faith.
    - Most hopeless before we find our hope.
    - Most alone before we find love.
- The best thing in life is FREE, His Grace!
- **The Frailty of Man** (initially published in *Navigating Life's Journey*)

  The pressure that results from adversity reveals our character.

  We all fail under pressure some of the time;
  Some of us fail under pressure all of the time.
  Thankfully, we all don't fail under pressure all of the time;
  Those successes under pressure build our society and forge progress.

- In relationships, there are takers and givers.
  - o When two takers connect, the result is ashes.
  - o When a taker and giver connect, the taker consumes the giver.
  - o When two givers connect, the fire burns forever.

Freedom Bullets

- Freedom is not only a state of existence and an American right, it is a muscle that we must regularly exercise to strengthen for the tough times we all face in life.
- There is no liberty when the government pursues equity as it proactively manipulates results in a vain attempt to achieve equality of outcomes. And, there is no individual liberty without economic and political freedom.
- The founder's views on freedom and power are as accurate today as then, which means the government they created will still have citizens, masters, over it if we dare to restrain the government's efforts to master the people.
- Slavery to anyone or anything is unacceptable. Preserving our freedom and passing it on to future generations is paramount.
- The patriots correctly understood the inherent nature of humans. The relevancy of their thoughts and writings confirms the immutable agelessness of human nature and reaffirms the brilliance contained in the Constitution and Declaration of Independence. The Constitution is not a breathing document that follows changes in human development but a solid foundation constraining the worst tendencies of humans to enslave people through government because human nature has not, nor will not, change.
- Consensus is the absence of leadership.
- A market economy is imperfect but significantly more beneficial to the people than a bureaucrat-managed one.
- Citizens leading citizens better serve us than professional politicians ruling subjects.
- Why would we throw away what has worked very well, though imperfectly, for what the millions who rush to America at the earliest opportunity can't escape quickly enough?
- It is WE THE PEOPLE who make America, not the government!

- AmeriCANS lead us to victory and achievement. AmeriCANT'S lead us to defeat and dishonor!
- Pursuing individual dreams creates national greatness through Adam Smith's invisible hand while pursuing collectivist dreams creates servants only to the elite rulers!
- No leader devoted to collectivism will respect an individual's freedom of speech and religion, private property, and the right to self-defense.
- Only leaders committed to individual liberty will honor those rights for citizens.
- Feckless leaders can serve undetected in good times, but when adversity strikes, their incompetence exponentially magnifies the damage incurred.
- What 100 years from now look like depends on what we do today.
- What we have now is Government:
  - by the career politicians.
  - for the career lobbyists.
  - executed by the career bureaucracy.
  - protected by the career media. Only breaking apart this syndicate will return liberty to the citizens.
- For the criminal, no law is sufficient. For the law-abiding, no law is needed.
- Consensus is not leadership; it is groupthink.
- Control what you can control. Adapt to what you can't control. Learn the difference.
- Characters in The Bible tell us we will all occasionally fail in life. It also reveals how we should respond to benefit humanity.
- Hope, Optimism, Personal growth, and Encouragement are the four horsemen of success.
- When we pursue our dreams utilizing our unique gifts combined with our fellow citizens, we repay the life we received and pass it along to future generations.

- The most underrepresented group in every legislative body is the taxpayer.
- As government grows at unabated warp speed, our individual liberties vanish as quickly.
- We, the people, get the freedom we demand and earn. When we surrender our independence, we get the government only too happy to dictate everything in our lives.
- To remain free, we must resist government's siren call to "take care of us."
- The government's end is always to seize power and grow, continually at the price of us ceding our independence and liberty.
- Our individual liberty is the paramount threat to government power and growth.
- There is no triumph in life without individual liberty and passing it to future generations.
- The only science that matters in Washington is political science.
- Absent freedom, peace is slavery.
- The answer to restoring our principles and exceptional culture is a return to the complete adherence to the founding doctrines, eliminating career politicians, and less government, not more.

APPENDIX C

SAGE SAYINGS FOR AmeriCANS

135 Sage Sayings: Good Enough to live by yesterday, and good enough to live by tomorrow.

Growing up, I heard wise old sayings from my parents, grandparents, great-grandmother, and other relatives and adults. Little did I know how sensible they were at the time.

Today, I rarely hear any of them anywhere. It is a shame because these phrases are as applicable today as previously, even though we may not understand where or when the expressions came into our culture.

This list contains astute sayings I have assembled over the years, but I acknowledge the list is incomplete. I'm unaware of the sources of most of them, which is why I haven't credited them.

I include them in this volume with the humble wish they be preserved and reintroduced to generations that will benefit from them.

A bird in the hand is worth two in the bush.
A chain is only as strong as its weakest link.
A day late and a dollar short.
A fool and his money are soon parted.
A penny saved is a penny earned. – Benjamin Franklin
A picture is worth a thousand words.
A rotten apple spoils the whole barrel.

A stitch in time saves nine.

A watched pot never boils. – Benjamin Franklin

Actions speak louder than words.

After everything is said and done, there is a lot more said than done.

All foam and no beer.

All for one and one for all. – Alexandre Dumas

All good things come to an end. – Geoffrey Chaucer

All good things in time.

All talk and no action.

All's fair in love and war.

An idle mind is the devil's workshop.

An ounce of prevention is worth a pound of cure. – Benjamin Franklin

Any friend of yours is a friend of mine.

Bad news rides a fast horse.

Better safe than sorry. – Samuel Lover

Blood is thicker than water.

Build a better mousetrap, and the world will beat a path to your door. – Ralph Waldo Emerson

Don't bite the hand that feeds you.

Don't change horses in the middle of a stream. – Abraham Lincoln

Don't cut off your nose in spite of your face.

Don't let the grass grow under your feet.

Don't make a mountain out of a molehill. – John Fox

Don't put all of your eggs in one basket.

Don't put the cart before the horse. – John Heywood

Don't throw good money after bad!

Don't throw the baby out with the bathwater.

Early to bed and early to rise, make a man healthy, wealthy, and wise. – Ben Franklin

Even the blind hog finds an acorn every once in a while.

Every dog has its day. – William Shakespeare

Every little bit helps.

Experience is the best teacher. – Frances M. Whitcher

Familiarity breeds contempt. – Geoffrey Chaucer

Flattery will get you everywhere. – Mae West

Fool me once; shame on you. Fool me twice; shame on me. – Anthony Weldon

Forewarned is forearmed. – J. Arderne

Good as gold.

Haste makes waste.

He who laughs last laughs best. – John Heywood

Hell hath no fury like a woman scorned. – William Congreve

Hindsight is 20-20.

Honesty is the best policy. – Benjamin Franklin

Hope springs eternal. – Alexander Pope

How can I hear what you say when what you do speaks so loudly?

If at first you don't succeed, try, try again. – Thomas H. Palmer

It is always darkest before the dawn. – Thomas Fuller

If it ain't broke, don't fix it.

If something sounds too good to be true, it probably is.

If the shoe fits, wear it.

If you can't stand the heat, get out of the kitchen. – President Harry S. Truman

If you lie down with dogs, you'll wake up with fleas. – Miguel de Cervantes

If you want a job done right, do it yourself.

If you want to know what is happening, FOLLOW THE MONEY.

Ignorance is bliss. – Thomas Gray

I'm so tired that I'm breathing from memory.

I'm working harder than the third monkey on the gangplank of Noah's ark.

Imitation is the sincerest form of flattery. – Charles Caleb Colton

It doesn't cost anything to be nice.

It's the thought that counts.

Lead, follow or GET OUT OF THE WAY! – George S. Patton

Let sleeping dogs lie. Leave well enough alone. – Geoffrey Chaucer

Look before you leap. – Samuel Butler

Make hay while the sun shines. – John Heywood

Many hands make work light.

Measure twice, cut once. – John Florio

Mind your p's and q's.

Necessity is the mother of invention. – Richard Franck

Never look a gift horse in the mouth. – John Heywood

Never put off until tomorrow what you can do today. – Benjamin Franklin

Never trouble trouble till trouble troubles you.

No news is good news. – James Howell

Nothing good ever happens after midnight.

Nothing ventured, nothing gained. – Benjamin Franklin

One bad apple spoils an entire barrel.

Pennywise and pound foolish. – Robert Burton

Perception is reality. – Lee Atwater

Poorer than Job's turkey.

Put your money where your mouth is.

Right beats might.

Rome wasn't built in a day. – John Heywood

Six of one or a half dozen of the other.

Sleep tight, and don't let the bed bugs bite.

Some day our ship will come in.

Some days you eat the bear, and some days the bear eats you.

Some days you're the pigeon, and some days you're the statue.

Some days you're the windshield, and some days you're the bug.

Sticks and stones may break my bones, but words will never hurt me.

Talk is cheap.

That's water under the bridge.

That which doesn't kill us makes us better.

The best-laid plans of mice and men often go awry. – Robert Burns

The bigger they are, the harder they fall. – Robert Fitzsimmons

The early bird gets the worm. – John Ray

The road to hell is paved with good intentions. – Henry G. Bohn

The squeaky wheel gets the grease. – Cal Stewart

There is an exception to every rule.

There is safety in numbers.

There's a sucker born every minute. – P. T. Barnum / And, two born to take him. – Bill Battle

There's more than one way to skin a cat. – Seba Smith

There's no place like home. – L. Frank Baum

There's no use crying over spilt milk.

Things aren't always as they appear.

Time is money. – Benjamin Franklin

Too many cooks in the kitchen spoils the broth.

Truth is stranger than fiction. – Mark Twain

Turnabout is fair play.

Two heads are better than one.

Two wrongs don't make a right.

Waste not, want not.

We might as well; we can't dance.

Well done is better than well said. – Benjamin Franklin

What goes around comes around. – Paul Crump

When in Rome, do as the Romans do. – Robert Burton

When it rains, it pours.

When you assume you make an ass out of you and me. – Oscar Wilde

Where there's a will, there's a way.

Where there's smoke, there's fire.

Why put off until tomorrow that which you can do today? – Benjamin Franklin

Winners never cheat, and cheaters never win.

Work is good for the soul.

You can lead a horse to water, but you can't make him drink.

You can't always get what you want. – Rolling Stones

You can't cheat an honest man. – W.C. Fields

You get what you pay for.

You learn something new every day!

You never get a second chance to make a good first impression.

You sound like you have been pulled through a knothole. – Chester Goode on *Gunsmoke*

Your day will come.

APPENDIX D

New Year's Resolutions
Good for Every Year

The following resolution principles can be selected and complemented with specific goals. The list is comprehensive enough to cover most objectives and general enough to utilize every year.

1. Be **Thankful** for what I have. His **Provision** always exceeds my need.
2. Be **Hopeful** in the new year.
3. Be **Fearless** and **Persevere** to **Overcome Obstacles.** Be a **Good Example** to others.
4. Be **Faithful** to my creator.
5. **Act Honorably.**
6. **Forgive** others who ask me to forgive them.
7. **Love** my neighbor as myself.
8. **Endure** setbacks.
9. **Encourage** others in the pursuit of their dreams.
10. Be **Trustworthy.**
11. Speak objective **Truth.**
12. Seek **Wisdom.**
13. **Stand Firm** through life's storms.
14. **Grow** personally every day.
15. Exercise **Patience** with others.
16. Pray for **Mercy** and **Rejoice** in **Grace.**
17. Live in **Peace** and **Good cheer.**

18. Be **Humble** when **Victorious.**
19. Have **Courage** in my **Heart** to live in **Joy.**

Principles taken from *Life's Daily Treasure: 366 Doses of Hope, Optimism, Personal growth, and Encouragement* by **Richard V. Battle. © 2021**

Index

RICHARD V. BATTLE
MULTI AWARD-WINNING AUTHOR,
SPEAKER, AND ADVISOR

Richard has previously authored *Life's Daily Treasure: 366 Doses of Hope, Optimism, Personal growth, and Encouragement, Navigating Life's Journey: Common Sense in Uncommon Times, Conquering Life's Course – Common Sense in Chaotic Times, Unwelcome Opportunity: Overcoming Life's Greatest Challenges, The Master's Sales Secrets, The Four-Letter Word that Builds Character, Surviving Grief by God's Grace,* and *The Volunteer Handbook: How to Organize and Manage a Successful Organization.*

He has been a public speaker and trainer for over 30 years on topics including leadership, motivation, faith, sales, and volunteerism.

Richard was an executive with **KeyTrak** (a Reynolds and Reynolds company) and has more than 40 years of experience in sales, executive management, and leadership in various business entities.

He was **appointed by Texas Governor Rick Perry** to **The Texas Judicial Council** and **The Texas Emerging Technology Fund**.

During his tenure as president of the **Austin Junior Chamber of Commerce**, the U.S. Junior Chamber of Commerce recognized the chapter as the Most Outstanding chapter in the United States, and the **Junior Chamber of Commerce International recognized Richard as the Outstanding Chapter President in the world**.

He served on the board of directors of **Alpha Kappa Psi**, an international professional business fraternity, and was a past chairman.

He has served on the board of many organizations including **The John Ben Shepperd Public Leadership Foundation,**

Boy Scouts of America, Muscular Dystrophy Association, and **Keep Austin Beautiful.**

Richard lives in Texas. His mission is to communicate timeless positive messages of proven principles helping people win every day.

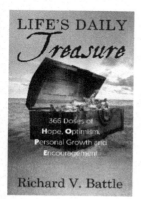

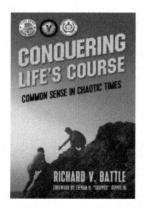

Conquering Life's Course
Common Sense in Chaotic Times

Do you wonder if Common Sense is vanishing? It will entertain and inspire the reader to think, laugh, and undertake actions to realize a more fulfilling life. If you or a loved one have given up on understanding the world of today, *Conquering Life's Course* is a must read. It offers reassurance to the reader that age-old traditions and wisdom still rule over unproven theory. It is concise, easy-to-read and offers invaluable insights that can be shared with the whole family. Available in paperback, Kindle, and audio editions.

Unwelcome Opportunity –
Overcoming Life's Greatest Challenges

What do you do when you experience divorce, two heart procedures, and a cancer diagnosis within ten months? It is the story of an ordinary man facing multiple life challenges in a ten-month period. In it, you will see an example of God's presence and provision that helped Richard Battle traverse this turbulent period of his life. Available in paperback, Kindle, Nook, and audio editions.

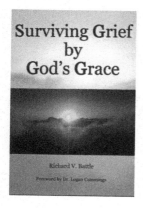

Surviving Grief by God's Grace

There is no greater loss in this world than the loss of one's child. This book is the first-person account of the author's loss of his first and then only child. It is a story of the grief, spiritual quest, and grace that helped Richard and his family survive and live with hope for the future. Available in paperback and Kindle editions.

The Four-Letter Word That Builds Character

Why are so many young people having a problem adapting to society today? Where have we gone wrong? Is it the parents or society in general? The Four-Letter Word That Builds Character can make a difference in this scattered and cluttered world. Based on the lessons learned from the author's first job and parental teaching of traditional values that have proven to be the foundation for lifelong success, this volume teaches 14 proven principles of a good work ethic and character. Available in paperback Kindle and audio editions.

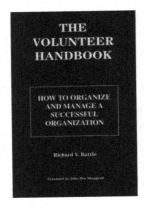

The Volunteer Handbook
How to Organize and Manage a Successful Organization

More than 75 topics that provide specific ideas that will help volunteer leaders maximize their efforts. Topics include: Long range, annual and event planning. Training board and prospective board members. How to recruit new members. 10 steps to activate or reactivate a member. 6 steps to building a successful team. How to motivate your membership. Effective delegation. Managing non-performers. Available in paperback.

The Master's Sales Secrets
44 Strategies for Sensational Sales Success

Richard V. Battle offers business leaders a graduate-level class in what he's learned in forty-plus years in sales and sales management. Practical, sharp, and clearly communicated, The Master's Sales Secrets can be read cover to cover or referenced strategy by strategy. Available in paperback and Kindle editions

www.richardbattle.com